22238

A Skills-based  inting

Painting
is a Class Act

This book is due for return on or before the last date shown below

6

Property of the School of ECLS Resource Centre
Newcastle University
Ring 0191 222 7569 to renew

Brilliant
PUBLICATIONS

We hope you and your pupils enjoy using the ideas in this book. Brilliant Publications publishes many other books for teaching art and design. To find out more details on any of the titles listed below, please log onto our website: www.brilliantpublications.co.uk.

Painting is a Class Act, Years 1–2	978-1-905780-29-7
Painting is a Class Act, Years 3–4	978-1-905780-30-3
Drawing is a Class Act, Years 1–2	978-1-903853-60-3
Drawing is a Class Act, Years 3–4	978-1-903853-61-0
Drawing is a Class Act, Years 5–6	978-1-903853-62-7
100+ Fun Ideas for Art Activities	978-1-905780-33-4
Preschool Art	978-1-897675-49-6
Discovering Great Artists	978-1-903853-16-0
The Big Messy Art Book	978-1-903853-18-4

Acknowledgements

I would like to thank the following primary schools for their permission to include in the publication examples of work by children in their schools. This work has been done over a number of years. Wherever work is named, permission was sought for inclusion.

Primary schools

Clovelly Primary School	Berrynarbor VC Primary School	Filleigh Community Primary School
Landscove Primary School	Witheridge C of E Primary School	

Individual pupil list

Alannah Stenning	Daniel Huxtable	James Newell	Marle Baxter
Amy Webber	Danny Hudson	Jason Witheridge	Megan Widlake
Andrew Newton	David Owens	Jay Latham	Millie Squire
Anthony Scott	Ebony Thorne	Jay Jury	Rita Roberts
Aran Goldsmith	Emily Hewitt	Jeff Hewitt	Rob Steel
Archie Muirhead	Emmie Perham	Jordan Hopkins	Simon Green
Beth Stewart	Francis Zoat	Jordan Wild	Sita Patel
Bethany Green	George Green	Joshua Derbyshire	Tabitha Waldon
Catherine Dixon	Giles Peacock	Joss Warren	Tamsin Cook
Clair Wyatt	Hayley Henry	Joyce Horridge	Thomas Corras
Claudia Dixon	Hettie Pearson	Karen Facey	Tom Murphy
Connor Wisken	Holly Peacock	Kelly White	Tom Worsley
Daisy Barker	Holly Stone	Kingsley Lerwill	Will Ayres
Daisy Perham	Izzy Merlin	Laura Denzy	William Taylor-Jones
Daisy Waldron	Jack Perham	Laura Gray	Zoe Elder

Published by Brilliant Publications
Unit 10
Sparrow Hall Farm
Edlesborough
Dunstable
Bedfordshire
LU6 2ES, UK

Website: www.brilliantpublications.co.uk

General information enquiries:
Tel: 01525 222292

The name Brilliant Publications and the logo are registered trademarks.

Written by Meg Fabian
Designed by Bookcraft Limited
Front cover designed by Brilliant Publications

© Text Meg Fabian 2010
© Design Brilliant Publications 2010

Printed: ISBN 978-1-905780-31-0
eBook: ISBN 978-1-85747-127-7

First printed and published in the UK in 2010

The right of Meg Fabian to be identified as the authors of this work has been asserted by herself in accordance with the Copyright, Designs and Patents Act 1988.

Pages 56, 65 and 120–128 may be photocopied by individual teachers acting on behalf of the purchasing institution for classroom use only, without permission from the publisher and without declaration to the Publishers Licensing Society. The materials may not be reproduced in any other form or for any other purpose without the prior permission of the publisher.

Foreword

Being able to paint is a life-enhancing skill and the development of painting skills has benefits far beyond the art lesson. Painting:

* helps children to express themselves
* helps to promote high standards in other areas of the curriculum
* raises children's self-esteem and confidence
* gives children an understanding and awareness of colour which can be life enhancing.

This book will be invaluable to non-specialist teachers as it clearly:

* sets out the development of painting skills
* offers guidance on progression
* provides ideas to support classroom activities.

Meg Fabian is the ideal person to write this book. She is a specialist with a passion for art and has been instrumental in raising children's standards and confidence in art across a range of North Devon schools.

Phil Creek
Adviser for Art and Design
Devon Education Services

Contents

Acknowledgements   2
Foreword   3
A skills-based approach to painting   6
Progression   8
Resources   10
Classroom organization   16
Starting points and ideas for themes, topics or inspiration   19

	Type of lesson	Time needed	Page
Basic skills			
Introducing powder paint			22
Investigating paintbrushes and brush strokes	Key Skill	1 hour	24
Using different brush strokes in a painting	Using Skill	30 min	25
Powder paint handling	Key Skill	30 min	26
Naming paint colours	Skill	20 min	27
Painting a picture in powder paint	Using Skill	1 hour	28
Making a colour lighter without using white: changing tone in colour (method 1)	Key Skill	20 min	29
Making a colour lighter without using white: dragging the colour (method 2)	Skill	15 min	30
Using the technique of dragging the colour to make a colour lighter	Using Skill	1 hour	31
Colour mixing			
Mixing colours			33
Recording colour mixing	Skill	45 min	34
Working in two blues	Skill	45 min	35
Mixing and recording colours: browns	Skill	45 min	36
Mixing and painting in browns	Using Skill	45 min	37
Mixing secondary colours	Key Skill	2 hours	38
Painting in secondary colours	Using Skill	1 hour	39
Changing one colour into another	Skill	45 min	40
Changing and blending colours by adding a little paint at a time	Skill	45 min	41
Making a collage using work from the previous lesson	Using Skill	1 hour	42
Making a collage using work from the previous lesson (simpler version)	Using Skill	1 hour	44
Making and using black paint	Skill	20 min	45
Adding black to make darker colours	Skill	Activity 1: 30 min Activity 2: 1 hour	46
Mixing greys	Skill	45 min	47
Mixing and painting only in greys	Using Skill	45 min	48
Creating skin tones	Skill	30 min	49
Painting a portrait using skin tones	Using Skill	1–2 hours	50
Colour matching	Skill	1 hour	51
Using a range of colours in a painting	Using Skill	1 hour	52
Colour theory			
Background information			54
Key aspects of colour theory			56
The colour wheel	Key skill	45 min	57
The extended colour wheel	Key skill	1 hour	58
Recording tones in colour on a colour wheel	Skill	1 hour	59
Revisiting and extending knowledge of colour theory	Using Skill	1 hour	60
Earth colours	Skill	1 hour	61
Painting using colour theory	Using Skill	1 hour	62
Trying out different colour combinations	Skill	1 hour	63

	Type of lesson	Time needed	Page

Colour theory (cont.)
Developing an awareness of tone in colour	Skill	1 hour	64
Assessing knowledge of colour and colour theory			65

Watercolours
Introduction to watercolours			67
Getting to know the colours and the box layout	Skill	30 min	69
How to use watercolours and how to make lighter colours without using white	Skill	30 min	70
Painting in lighter and darker tones of watercolours	Using Skill	1 hour	71
Painting a 'wash'	Key Skill	30 min	72
Painting a simple landscape with a wash background	Using Skill	30 min	73
Colour mixing in watercolours	Skill	i hour	74
Colour mixing and varying the tone in watercolours	Using Skill	1–2 hours	75
Painting drawings using a restricted palette	Using Skill	45 min	76
Using colour theory to create the illusion of distance	Skill	45 min	77
Colour mixing with watercolour coloured pencils	Skill	45 min–1 hour	78

Acrylics
Introducing acrylic paints			80
Using acrylic paints	Skill	30 min	82
Acrylic paints	Using Skill	2 hours	83
Painting exterior walls with acrylic paints: a long-term large-scale project	Using Skill	Stage 1: 30–40 min	84
		Stage 2: 15min per child	
		Stage 3: 30min per child	

Oils
An introduction to oil paints			86
Using oil paints	Skill	1 hour	88
Painting in oils	Using Skill	2 hours	89

History of painting
A few key pointers in the history of painting			91
A timeline of colours			93
Cave paintings, part 1: making your own paint and charcoal	Skill	1 hour	94
Cave paintings, part 2 (can be done with or without making your own paint, brushes and charcoal)	Skill	1 hour	95
Egyptian painting	Skill	2 hours	96
Medieval art: illuminated letters	Skill	2 hours	97

Using works of art
Artists and art movements			99
Questioning that will enhance children's responses to and understanding of works of art			104
Using a painting by Van Gogh	Skill	3 hours or more	106
Using a painting by Seurat (spatter technique: session 1)	Skill	2 hours	107
Using a painting by Seurat (spattered paper: session 2)	Skill	3 hours or more	108

Other techniques and media
Other methods of applying paint			110
Line and wash	Skill	45 min	111
Aborigine dreamtime pictures	Skill	1 hour	112
Blow paintings	Skill	1 hour	113

Assessment
Assessment of painting			115
Pupils' self-assessment			116

Bibliography			116
Glossary			117
Resource sheets			120

A skills-based approach to painting

For children as young artists, painting can be a means of personal expression, a way to express ideas and feelings.

All artists experiment with colour and use materials in a personal way. This book aims to enable teachers to support children in this same process of discovery and exploration.

The use of paint needs to be taught to children; they need to be led to an awareness of colour and how it can be mixed and used in order for them to grow in confidence and in understanding in the handling of paint. They should know it can be applied in layers or changed, and that its surface can be flat or textured. They should know that different qualities of paint may be used for different purposes.

Younger pupils will generally paint without inhibition, but as children progress through the school they will need direct teaching in order for them to master the media and to develop skills. The originality, the individual vision and inspiration will come from them. However formally they are taught, their creativity will not be impaired and they will still evolve their own style and have their own ideas.

How the skills-based approach works
Painting is essentially about colour and paints and the way in which these are controlled and used. In this book, these aspects are taken apart and pared down to their basic elements. They have been separated initially into simple lessons which show children how particular types of paint behave and the different ways in which colours can be mixed and used.

The skills acquired should be used in a context as soon as possible, not only for purposes of consolidation, but also so that children will be able to see how these skills can be used in a painting and how they will increase the effectiveness of their work.

James Newell, Year 5

The skills and experiences should build over time to help children develop the confidence and competence they need to create the effects they desire. They should to be able to express their own ideas and feelings effectively in paint and colour. Confidence in the process and in themselves is essential if they are going to gain the benefits of being able to take pleasure in it and communicate through this medium.

One way to achieve this confidence is to help children achieve control over the paints and the tools. They should also be encouraged to see opportunities to change and develop their work when they use these skills in the context of a painting.

Children need to realize that adult artists also had to learn and practise basic techniques and that they themselves are now involved in the same process.

Learning to paint is as difficult as learning any other complex discipline. One way we can help children not to be overwhelmed with the task is to limit the choices of media and colours, and to be specific about the focus of the painting session.

Paints have different properties and children should be given experience of a wide range, although they should not be introduced to too many at once because this will confuse them. It is to be recommended that the school has one staple paint medium that will be used consistently throughout the school, with other painting media being used alongside this as appropriate.

Children's skills will develop more successfully if the teacher introduces painting tools and media systematically, and encourages children to experiment, whilst providing learning tasks that are challenging. In this way, it is possible to build their skills and confidence step by step until they are equipped to launch out on their own with less and less teacher intervention.

In this book, the staple paint is powder paint, with ready-mixed paint figuring mainly with the younger age groups. However, a wide range of other painting media are introduced at various stages throughout the book.

Looking at the work of other artists to see how they have dealt with colour and paint is an integral part of this approach to the teaching of painting. It helps children to recognize that they are young artists struggling with the same essential elements of painting – colour, shape, tone, texture and movement – as all adult artists, past and present.

When looking at works of art, they can be told, 'This is what artists do. They look at each other's work for inspiration and solutions, and they take ideas and change them. This is what they have always done; it is why artists often like to work and live near other artists. A creative person can take an idea and turn it into something which is his or her own.'

Few children in a school will become professional artists, but an appreciation of art and of colour is life-enhancing.

Hayley Henry, Year 5

Progression

In an ideal world, there would be consistency and continuity in the approach to painting throughout the school. The order of the content of the art curriculum will vary according to the school's own planning, but the principle behind the teaching in this book is that the skill/medium/technique is introduced and taught and is then used in a painting context as soon as possible. This could be the same day, the next art session, or whenever is appropriate to the skill.

Children will need regular opportunities to experiment with a new medium so that they have a chance to examine its potential. Successful use of a new skill or medium boosts a child's self-esteem and builds confidence to experiment.

Whereas there are some media that are more age-appropriate than others (for example, oil painting is generally better saved for older Key Stage 2 children), it is as well, where possible, to give all ages the opportunity to experiment with different media and materials. Older junior children can make stunning mono prints from finger paintings, whilst young infants respond well to the challenge of painting with tiny brushes.

Painting should be tackled in terms of what is possible and appropriate to the medium. Learning about paint is a gradual process, beginning in school at the foundation stage and developing in complexity as understanding grows.

This should be enhanced from the earliest years by the introduction of works of art. Children should be invited to respond and to develop a vocabulary of response. The questioning from the teacher should become more probing and specific as the years go by, starting with simple questioning about what the children can see and what they like or don't like about a work of art, and progressing to such thoughts as 'what the artist's intention might have been'.

Examples of a range of questioning in response to works of art is to be found on page 104 in the chapter on Using works of art.

Children's development in painting

Children first use colour at an intuitive and emotional or convenience level, because they like it, because it looks right or because it was handy and there was some left.

Children tend to express what they know rather than what they see, which is why skies tend to be blue at the top of the page and grass green at the bottom, with an area of white left in between. The appearance of a yellow quarter section of a sun in the top right- or left-hand corner is really just a symbol which the child knows will be recognized and 'read' by whoever views the painting. They become quite surprised if they are questioned about why they put it there and when they last saw a sun like this.

This schematic approach to painting a scene should really not appear later than Year 3, unless the child is very immature, as then it is really just a form of laziness. As they mature, they become more aware of the complexity of the visual environment and the problems of interpreting the 'real' world.

When children become aware of the difference between the images they paint and those they

Year 6 pupil

see around them, they can lose satisfaction with what they have produced and it becomes important to them that their images are acceptable to others as well as themselves.

As young children develop an awareness of space, the random earlier daubs are replaced by a more considered representation. At this stage there is no concept of scale and the child exaggerates and distorts to emphasize things of personal significance and importance. As co-ordination increases, children extend their range of symbols and execute paintings with more detail, together with a diminishing size of their work.

Experience and progression of skills

Year 5

* Chooses appropriate media and tools for work
* Works increasingly independently
* Works with care and precision showing control over media
* Revises colour theory and understands how colours react to each other
* Tests colour theory in own paintings
* Sets challenge: 'can you make some things look further away or closer in your picture just by using colour rather than scale?'
* Creates and compares different shades of grey and white
* Develops background and works on own pre-prepared backgrounds
* Extends knowledge of how artists use colour theory to create certain effects
* Uses acrylics to create texture to paintings
* Learns rules of classic composition in landscape
* Looks at symbolism in works of art
* Develops a piece of work from a sketch and notes, through various stages of modification to finished piece of work
* Evaluates own and others' work using subject-appropriate vocabulary
* Considers different ways to develop or extend or change a painting
* Lays a colour wash in watercolours and paints a simple monochrome scene over the top, working wet and dry
* Paints on a variety of surfaces inside a building, as well as outside in appropriate materials
* Uses secondary resources to get ideas
* Creates skin tones in different paints
* Extends art vocabulary to include techniques, terms and art movements

* Understands conventions of still life painting and the symbolism
* Looks at the role of religion in the history of painting
* Considers the impact of photography on artists 150+ years ago
* Uses appropriate vocabulary to describe design process
* Studies significant changes in the development of painting, from cave paintings to the present day, by looking at key works of art
* Works both individually and in groups
* Visits a gallery
* Meets a professional artist.

Also by the end of Year 6
* Creates paintings in different genres (eg still life, landscape, portrait) in a variety of media
* Revisits colour theory and identifies its use in works of art
* Extends range of colour mixing in watercolours, creating subtle colours
* Works in a very small scale with tiny brushes, eg Indian miniatures
* Paints from close observation using colour matching skills
* Paints a watercolour study which includes a wash and over-painting
* Uses oils colours and works on canvas
* Experiments with line and wash
* Develops own style in painting
* Paints scenes showing scale, distance, form and space, juxtaposition and overlapping
* Creates illusion of distance in a painting
* Explores the effect of light in a painting
* Uses skills, colours, tools and effects to represent something observed, remembered or imagined
* Continues to use sketchbooks to record observations and to collect images for later use in paintings.

Jordan Hopkins, Year 5

Resources

In an ideal world, a well-stocked art cupboard might contain:

Different types of paint
* Ready-mixed
* Powder paint
* Tempera paint (blocks and tablets)
* Watercolours (blocks in tins)
* Watercolours: powdered (Brusho®)
* Poster paint
* Metallic
* Pearlescent
* Cromar
* Fabric paint
* Acrylic
* Gouache
* Marbling
* Emulsion (for large-scale work)

Drawing media
* Watercolour pencils
* Water-soluble crayons
* Charcoal
* Oil pastel
* Art (chalky) pastels
* Felt tips
* Permanent ink pens

Brushes
* Long- and short-handled stiff-bristled brushes in different sizes and tips
* Watercolour brushes in various sizes
* Decorator brushes in various sizes

Papers
As well as the usual paper that a primary school keeps:
* Cartridge paper, ready-cut in various sizes
* Kitchen paper
* Junior art paper
* Thin card (for acrylics)
* Blotting paper

Sundry items
* Brush holders
* Paint wells (for powder paint)
* Sketchbooks
* Palettes (various types to suit the paint being used)
* Water pots
* Protective clothing
* Painting storage racks (for drying)
* Masking tape

Technical painting terms

The painter's materials are called 'media' and include, for example, oils, watercolours, acrylics, etc.

These media are applied to a 'support', such as canvas, wood, paper, using a variety of tools such as brushes, palette knife and fingers. Below the surface of a painting there may be other layers of paint, usually called an 'under-painting', and beneath the painting there may also be an 'under-drawing'.

Explanation of other painting terms can be found in the glossary on page 117.

Paints

Finger paints
These usually come ready-mixed in re-sealable pots; they are available in bright colours, in black and white and with glitter.

Ready-mixed
Ready-mixed paint comes in squeezy bottles. The same colours should be stocked as for powder paints: vermilion and crimson red, brilliant and cyan blue, lemon and brilliant yellow, and black and white.

Ready-mixed paint is not as good as powder paint for colour mixing, but it is very useful for larger-scale work for all ages and for painting models. Also, other substances can be added to it to create textured paint. More about this is on page 110 under 'Texture'.

It has its limitations for colour mixing as, the larger the range of colours you have, the more children will tend to dip into colours and use them straight from the bottle rather than mix their own. As with most paints, it is advisable to order double the quantity of white and yellow.

Metallic paint
It is better to buy this in ready-mixed form as the powdered variety can be difficult to mix up. There are two grades of ready-mixed paint: Meltdown paint, which is more expensive but is suited to smaller-scale work and is excellent for painting small clay models; and less expensive varieties which are not so glorious when dry but which are quite suitable for general use and for younger children.

Pearlescent

These water-based paints have a lovely shimmer and add a different dimension to a painting. They are also useful for painting models, and particularly for clay models if the school does not have a kiln to fire glazes.

Cromar

These are translucent water-based paints that can be used on any surface but are ideal for use on glass or plastic.

Tempera (block) paint

Tempera comes in solid blocks and needs to be thoroughly moistened before use. The blocks – flat cylindrical tablets that fit into a palette – need to be of a good quality, otherwise it is difficult to make paint of a covering consistency. They have limited use when colours need to be mixed as they generally end up with other colours over the top and have to be cleaned before they can be used next time. No lessons in this medium are included in this book.

Tempera paints are quick to set out and are not messy to clear up, so they can be useful when the classroom has no sink, and younger children do not find them daunting. However, they are not sufficient to be the only paint available.

Powder paint

Powder paint is the best painting medium in the primary school. It allows full and sensitive colour mixing and is reasonably priced. It comes in dry form and children can mix it themselves, but the process needs to be taught. The best aspect of powder paint is that it is possible to mix an almost limitless range of colours. It is not necessary to stock more than six colours plus black and white.

The downside of using powder paint is that it can be difficult for children to mix a large amount of a blended colour, and they need to develop their skills in using it. They will also need direct teaching and support to get the right consistency. There is more about this in the chapter on Basic skills (pages 22–23).

Watercolour

This comes in three forms: tablet, tube and powder. The tablets can be bought separately or ready placed in tins which have a lid that can be used for colour mixing. The tubes are more expensive and are really only suitable for older Key Stage 2 children who have had experience of working with tablets.

The powder is very versatile and is excellent for large washes, wax resist and for use on fabrics, especially batik. The most common brand is Brusho®. It is not colour-fast and will wash out. It can be mixed with water to any density of colour and can be stored in screw-top jars for later use. It can also be sprinkled directly onto damp paper for an unusual effect. It comes in small tubs and will stain the skin under your fingernails, so it is advisable to wear latex gloves when mixing it.

Watercolours become translucent when applied thinly.

Poster paint

This water-based paint comes in small pots or tubes and does not really do anything that good quality ready-mixed paint does not.

Fabric paint

There are a variety of fabric paints available from different suppliers. There are colour-fast varieties, and also some that come in crayon form. Some need ironing to make them colour-fast. They come in all colours, including fluorescent and pearlescent types.

Acrylic paint

Acrylic paint is a thick, creamy paint sold in large tubes or pots. Acrylics can be diluted with water but have a plastic base which forms a waterproof skin. The paint peels off skin but does not come out of clothes, and for this reason it is not really suitable for Key Stage 1 use unless the children are closely supervised.

Acrylic paint can be built up in layers, can be over-painted once dry without mixing colours, and can be used to create texture. It can be applied with a brush or a palette knife.

Particular care has to be taken when using acrylic paint as it is also a strong adhesive. Paintbrushes need to be cleaned immediately after the painting session has finished or they will set rock hard and have to be thrown away.

Oils

Despite its reputation as 'high art', oil painting is relatively simple. It is exciting for Year 6 children to try out and makes a good last-term-at-primary-school activity.

The paint needs to be used with white spirit or turps for thinning and for cleaning the brushes. Only six colours need to be purchased: Titanium white, Cadmium red, Cadmium yellow, Alizarin crimson, Ultramarine and Prussian blue. However, the range could be extended with Raw sienna, Burnt umber and Ivory black.

Gouache

Gouache is an opaque watercolour; the pigment is thickened with white chalk. It is not really necessary in primary school unless a particular project requires it, although it is a useful medium for graphic design. It comes in tubes.

Ink

Ink is a transparent dye. Inks come in beautiful colours for ink and wash work. However, you really only need black, although sepia is lovely to use. A little goes a long way. Brusho® (powdered watercolour) can be used in place of ink if it is mixed with only a small amount of water. Check the ink label to ensure that it is safe to use with children.

Marbling inks

Marbling inks are special oil-based colours. They float on the surface of water, and paper can be laid on top to pick up the patterns of the swirling colours. They are relatively foolproof and children love the effects created. However, the children need to wear protective clothing.

Emulsion paint

Household emulsion paint is good for large-scale work, internal murals or scenery. It is less expensive than ready-mixed paint and some types are wipeable.

Care needs to be taken that the instructions on the tin state that it is safe for children to use. Many children have very sensitive skins.

Drawing media

Watercolour pencils

These are artists' quality coloured pencils. Lovely colour blending effects can be achieved with them and the children's drawings can be wet with a brush so the colours move and blend. They are particularly useful in plant studies.

Water-soluble crayons

These are used in the same way as watercolour pencils.

Felt tips

Most felt-tip pens can be used as described for watercolour pencils. They are also interesting to use to show colour separation when spots of colour are drawn onto wet blotting paper and left for the colours to spread and separate.

Permanent ink pens

These generally come in three thicknesses, and the thicker points can be round- or chisel-ended.

These are excellent for drawing over paintings (examples of this can be seen on pages 6 and 75). They work well over watercolours, but care needs to be taken when using them over thick powder paint or ready-mixed paint, because the pen points can clog, and they do not work well over wet paint. Permanent pens are also good for drawing before painting, as the ink does not run when paint is applied over drawings.

Charcoal

Charcoal drawings can be wet with a brush and the black will move to make shades of grey. This is a classic medium and has a long history.

Artists' pastels

Chalky pastels can be used in the same way as charcoal. Using sepia or burnt sienna pastels can give an 'old look' to a painting. This might be appropriate when studying artists such as Leonardo da Vinci, for example.

Brushes

It is important to offer the children a range of brushes, both small and large. House painting brushes are also useful for covering large areas and for certain techniques such as spatter painting. Brushes need to be looked after, washed out after use and never stored brush-ends downward in a container. This is particularly important with short-handled watercolour brushes as these are virtually unusable once the ends have become bent. Store brushes which are to be used for acrylics and oils separately.

Children need to be taught good brush techniques, ie how to hold them just above the ferrule (metal band) with a similar hold to pencils, and not to scrub with them, which splays the hairs. This shortens their life (the brushes not the children, although if I catch them at it…!!).

Children should also be encouraged not to leave their brushes standing in water pots, but to rinse them and lay them across their palettes or on the table, even when the lesson is paused for further information and teaching. It is prudent to make this the normal practice so it becomes second nature. Brushes' points, particularly watercolour brush points, become misshapen when left standing in water.

Different brush strokes can be made with different ends. A range of good brushes in different sizes is essential if pupils are to be able to master the process of painting. Different media require different brushes.

General-use brushes: ready-mixed paint, powder and acrylics

Hog hair is the cheapest option and adequate for most uses; the downside is that they tend to be softer and can lose their hair. Synthetic hair is also available. This is more expensive, but it keeps its shape well and is more economical in the long run.

Brushes are generally long-handled and are available in a range of thicknesses from size 4 to size 18. The handle length is a matter of personal preference, having something to do with balance, but this really applies to adults. However, longer-handled brushes are easier to store upside-down in blocks or pots as the handles are slimmer than the shorter varieties.

For general use, the round ends are adequate, but it is important to have a range of sizes of the flat ends as well, particularly for using with acrylics and oil, and also for painting in textured paint. A brush with a square end will produce a different effect from a round one. In order to gain confidence in the use of a range of brushes, it is good to encourage pupils to experiment with their differing effects, recording the outcomes in their sketchbooks.

Watercolour brushes

The best brushes, like the best paints, tend to be the most expensive. The cheaper brushes are really not worth bothering with; they will just make it more difficult for children to achieve control over this tricky medium.

If the art budget will run to sable, get that type and then make sure the children value them and look after them. If not, then buy the best you can afford.

A range of sizes is again important, the smallest is size 0 and the range goes up to size 12. The larger ones are good for washes and the small to medium ones for detail.

Watercolour brushes need to be looked after and should be kept separately and stored with care – never brush-end downward in a pot.

Brush storage

There are ready-made brush stands available from different suppliers. It can be a bit fiddly to put the brushes in some of them, but this can always be done by an art monitor. Otherwise, cleaned brushes can be stored flat in trays or wooded ends down in pots in their different sizes.

Children should be encouraged to choose the most appropriate brush for the job in hand, particularly in terms of size. Frequently, children will try to cover large areas with a tiny brush or try to paint in minute detail with a large brush. If a range of brush sizes is available to them on their table from the onset of the session, they will be more likely to independently choose the best one for their purpose.

Other methods of paint application

It is important to point out that brushes are not the only method of applying paint to a surface. Most children enjoy inventing and making their own painting implements. There is an example of this on page 94 in the chapter on History of painting.

Children should, where possible, be given the opportunity to experiment with such things as fingers, sponges, rags, cotton buds, strips of card and rollers.

Twigs and feathers, rags and cotton wool can be used to lift off paint as well as apply it.

Paper

Shape

Artists have terms for which way round paper is to be used. 'Portrait' refers to having the long side vertical, while 'landscape' refers to the longer side being horizontal.

Quality

Good quality paper is essential if the paint is to adhere satisfactorily to the surface and if the paper is to remain flat after drying. If the paper is too thin, it may well not absorb moisture and may cockle when dry, spoiling the look of the work.

Paper is sold not only in sizes but also by weight. The weight of one square metre of paper in grams is written as GSM or g/sm: the larger the number, the stronger and firmer the paper. 70–170 g/sm is the range most school suppliers carry.

It is useful to order the paper you need in manageable sizes, unless you need the largest size for large-scale or group work. The very large sheets are difficult to store and often become damaged when other paper is removed or replaced. Separate packs of A1, A2, A3 and A4, ready-cut in the weight you need, are useful. Larger pieces have to be cut to size and there is not always enough time to fiddle about. As art is such a resource-heavy subject, collecting and setting out a range of media before a lesson can be daunting. Locating the guillotine, finding a space to put it on and cutting up the paper can be the last straw.

Sketchbooks should be of the best quality paper that the art budget can run to; not only is it better for drawing on but it will hold the paint and mean children can work directly into their books when necessary.

Types of paper

Kitchen paper

Thin, cheap paper, also known sometimes as 'fish and chip' paper, is not an ideal surface for paint. It goes soggy quickly, it cockles, and the colours disappear into it. It can be acceptable for early years work, but only because these children do so many paintings, sometimes consisting of just a few brush strokes. In this case it would be expensive to use good quality cartridge paper all the time.

Junior art paper

Junior art paper is slightly lighter and cheaper than cartridge paper and is adequate for general use. However if a lot of paint or paint with high water content is being used, cartridge is better.

Cartridge

Cartridge paper is so called because it was made strong and firm in order to make cartridges for gunpowder. 115 g/sm is a good medium weight for general use, while 135 g/sm is better for acrylics and watercolours.

Watercolour papers

Watercolour paper is expensive. It is rougher and stiffer than other papers, but it holds the paint well and won't bubble up when it is wetted. Children could practise skills on good quality cartridge and, when it comes to their final paintings, watercolour paper could be used.

Pre-prepared backgrounds

Backgrounds should not always be white, nor always plain. It is good to give the children the opportunity to paint on coloured, patterned and textured surfaces.

Backgrounds can be:
* Wet, damp or dry
* Screwed up and smoothed out
* Rollered, using printing or decorator's rollers, with paint or printing ink
* Collaged
* Painted
* Printed in different ways, eg screwed-up cling film, bubble wrap or fabric
* Colour-washed using thin paints or inks
* Textured, such as wallpaper, sandpaper or woodchip.

Canvas and canvas board

Most oil paintings are painted on canvas. This is usually a piece of linen cloth that has been stretched over a frame or board and then protected with a primer. Canvas board is cheaper, but nowadays small canvases can be purchased quite inexpensively at many high street outlets, and this may prove better value than art or school suppliers.

Other surfaces and finishes

Paint can be applied to many different surfaces, such as cardboard, chipboard, wood, stone, etc. Some surfaces, however, need specialist paint – ceramics and glass, for example, and also fabric if it is to be washed and the colours not fade.

Children could paint on walls, doors, benches, trees, on fabric or on plastic. Old shoes, containers and furniture can be transformed.

Clear PVA can be over-painted to make artwork waterproof (up to a point), or varnishes can be applied to make colours brighter. I have heard that furniture polish can be sprayed over powder paint paintings and then buffed to bring out the colours. However I have had no success with this; perhaps I am using the wrong polish!

Other resources

Water pots

Water pots need to be stable and stackable. The type with a wider base than top are the best, and also don't need a lid. The pots must be tall enough to hold long-handled brushes so that they don't fall out. You will need enough for one between two children and plenty of spares for other purposes, such as holding quantities of ready-mixed paint or mixed-up Brusho® (powdered watercolour).

Palettes

There are several different varieties of palettes available from suppliers, but many teachers just use old plates. It depends really upon what suits your purpose and what you personally prefer to use.

Palettes need to be easy to wash out quickly, so curved edges to the hollows are helpful. They also need to stack and not take up too much room on the table. Unless you are lucky enough to have an art room with lots of table space for each child, you will need to consider carefully the space on the table for paints, palettes, water pots and whatever other resources are being used.

Plastic moulded palettes with nine wells are excellent for colour mixing, as they give enough space for a range of colours and are big enough to share between two. Palettes are also available with six wells.

The disadvantage of mixing paint on single flat surfaces, like plates or trays, is that it is difficult to keep the colours separated and they tend to run together.

Watercolours can be mixed in the lids of the paint boxes, on an old plate, on palettes with smaller wells; a stiff piece of shiny card will do if you are really stuck.

It is possible to buy special paper palettes for oils and acrylics, and this may save a lot of time on clearing up.

A tip which saves water and washing-up time is to put a piece of cling film over the palette. At the end of the painting session, pull off the cling film and throw it away. This leaves the palettes clean and does not pour chemicals into the water system.

Easels
Children should have the experience of working at an easel at some stage in their school life. While it is good to be able to stand back from your work and view it at a distance, the disadvantage is that, unless it is very thick, the paint tends to run down the paper. Once the children have dipped their brushes in the water to clean them, the paint becomes thin and watery and will dribble down the page.

If you have a large art room, you might invest in a few collapsible easels which store easily. A group of older children could then try the experience of working, standing half an arm's length from the easel, and they could also try holding the paintbrush further along the handle than usual. This would really only be for suitable for oil, acrylic or thickened paints.

Drying racks
There are several different types available, pretty much all of them fiddly and tricky in different ways. The ones with loose, moveable shelves are particularly maddening as the shelves tend to come away in your hand when you are holding a wet painting in the other. Others have shelves which, after a few years of use, tend to slope downwards (children have been known to lean on them and speed this tendency), so inevitably the wet paintings all slide off the shelves. Fun!

Drying racks take up space in a classroom unless wall-mounted, and they can become dumping grounds; however, they are essential in order to have somewhere to put wet artwork and to stop it becoming dog-eared and damaged. If the racks are accessible to children, they can carry their own work to the rack, but this can be fraught with danger. Wet artwork often runs unless children remember to carry it horizontally, and there is always the danger of them bumping into a child who isn't wearing a painting overall, thereby smearing them with paint. This is naturally always a child who has a very particular parent!

Some drying racks have lift-up shelves, others have pull-out shelves, and some are on wheels so they can be removed from the classroom.

Pegging artwork up on washing lines or clothes drying racks is a popular solution and can work well unless paint is wet and running.

Protective clothing
This is another area fraught with difficulty, so here are a few suggestions.

An old adult-sized T-shirt makes an excellent painting overall. It has no buttons or strings and slips on easily. It covers most of the arms and the body, and comes down to the thighs or even lower. You could purchase 30 or so new T-shirts quite cheaply, probably at no more than a pound each, whereas you could spend the whole year asking children to bring them in from home and get only a few responses.

The school could buy painting overalls or aprons for each class, but it is only worthwhile getting the better quality ones, which can work out expensive. You would also need to get several different sizes, and upper Key Stage 2 children are not keen to wear them. Cheaper aprons, however, are a waste of time as they rip or split very quickly.

Whichever way you do it, the children need to protect their clothes for most painting lessons, although with watercolours it is not so important.

Classroom organization

The first consideration in classroom organization is, 'how many children are going to be painting at one time?' This determines how much equipment is needed. Sometimes children may paint in smaller groups, with the activity rotating over the day or week, until everyone that should have had a go at the activity has had their turn. However, it is quite likely that, for various reasons, there will be times when the whole class is painting at the same time.

The greater the number of children painting at the same time, the more crucial it is that the equipment is organized efficiently. Children can then achieve optimum benefit from the experience and will not have to battle against the mess and muddle that can ensue quickly when equipment is not organized with care and consideration.

Many teachers shudder at the thought of a whole class of young children all painting at the same time, but it is manageable and it does have some advantages. It provides a whole-class experience, and the shared sense of discovery

and achievement can be powerful. It does 'get it over with' in one go, and with such a crowded curriculum there is no longer time for things to drag out over several weeks. Also, with smaller groups each taking their own turn to paint, the moment can pass and the activity may lose its impact, or a topical aspect may no longer apply. There are also display implications: do you wait until all the children have done it before the artwork goes up on the wall?

The following are a few pointers that apply whatever the size of the group, and regardless of where the art materials are kept – whether they are in your classroom, stored in some central location or, if your school is big enough, in an art room.

Newspaper
If you cover tables with newspaper, two layers is best. The advantage of this is that it absorbs some spills, extra layers can be added if necessary and damp brushes can be dried on it. Newspaper can be cleared quickly away at the end of the session and, unless there have been a lot of spills, tables should not even need wiping. If the children are setting out newspaper themselves, then check that it does not poke out beyond the edges of the table. This can cause disasters in that, when anyone walks past the table, they are in danger of catching it against themselves and inadvertently swiping everything off of the table and onto the floor.

One last point about newspapers: broadsheets do the job best. It takes less time to lay them out as the pages are bigger and there are likely to be fewer 'unsuitable' images. Even then, keep an eye out for images that might distract children for whatever reason. Just flip those pages over.

Setting out tables
Consider paper size before setting out the tables; if children are working with A2 or A3 paper, then fewer of them can work at a time. If it is group work on a large-scale surface, you may have to leave space around the edge of the table for materials, or place them on a table nearby. Where there are implications for different media, these will be covered in the relevant lesson. Otherwise, for a table of children working on individual work, set out:

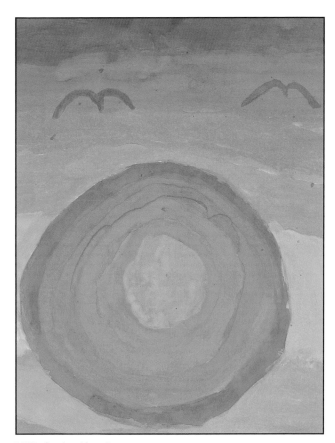

Millie Squire, Year 5

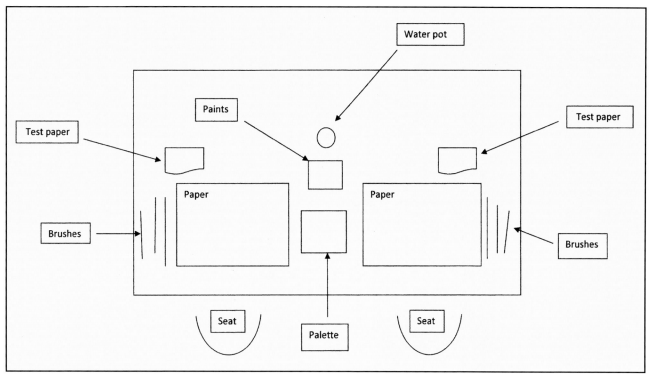

A table set out for two children

※ Paper for artwork
※ Enough water pots and paints and palettes positioned so that children do not have to reach across each other to get to them (this causes water and paint to land on their paintings when it shouldn't)
※ A test paper for each child to try out colours and dab brushes on
※ A pencil, for writing the child's name on the back of their work, if nothing else
※ At least one brush per child, or possibly a selection of brushes of different sizes, which is better to give children the opportunity to exercise choice.

As a general rule, one water pot and one palette between two children works well. This may vary according to the activity and the size of the palettes.

Consider what other resources need to be on the table, eg items to be depicted, other art media or sketchbooks and where they can be best placed. Sketchbooks take up a lot of room; if children are using these for reference, they could put them under their chairs while they are not looking at them.

Remember that children will also need protective clothing (see page 15).

There is more specific information about setting out different media in chapters relating to that particular medium.

Changing dirty paint water
Children should be encouraged to change their water when they think it needs changing. It can be explained to them that although their water may look dirty, it only needs changing if, when they put a clean brush in the water and then dab it onto their test paper, it shows up as a colour rather than just a wet mark. If it shows up as a colour, then tell them to change it.

Consideration for others
Children should have been encouraged to help set out, clear away and clean up from the earliest age, but they still may need reminding to keep their work space clean. If this becomes messy, not only is their own artwork in danger of getting ruined but so is other children's work. They need to be taught to look after the brushes and to consider the needs of other children who are sharing the materials.

Clearing up
Oh dear, the dreaded clearing-up time! This is not so bad if you have adult help, but for a number of reasons this may not be available. If you do not have a teaching assistant, or you do have one but they are not free to assist, a willing parent helper is a boon. Failing all these options, however, you will just have to pack up a bit earlier and have a simple activity organized to keep the children busy whilst you deal with the clearing up. It could be you at the sink or an adult helper.

Here are a few suggestions and a sequence of clearing-up activities:

* Have no more than four 'monitors'.
* Say, 'No one is to get up from their seats unless I have asked them to', otherwise the room will be full of children milling about with water pots, etc, getting in each other's way or getting into mischief.
* Clear up one group at a time and leave the others still working.
* Remove artwork first and put it somewhere safe. Clearing-up time is the most likely time for something disastrous to happen to it.
* Don't let any children carry powder paint around, because sooner or later they will drop it or will trip up and send it flying. It will go everywhere.
* Collect brushes and drop them into the sink (even if children have washed them, they will still generally need another wash). Leave them there while the water pots are rinsed.
* Collect the water pots next and wash them up, stacking them upside-down to drain. These take up the most room in the sink and so are best got rid of first.

* Wash the brushes and stand them to drain in a water pot or two.
* Collect palettes (or paint pots) and dump them in the sink to soak (NB see note about palettes and cling film on page 15).
* While the palettes are soaking, remove any other paint from the tables.
* Collect test papers.
* Remove newspaper.
* Send that group to wash their hands and put away their aprons, and give them their next activity.
* Wash the palettes, which, by now, will not be so difficult to clean. Children will need to be taught how to clean palettes. Getting the tap turned on at the right pressure is key to this, as is holding the palettes under running water at an angle away from themselves.
* Repeat the clearing-up routine with the next group.

This is not as bad as it sounds. If, whenever possible, the children have something to do, it should run fairly smoothly. There will be times when they will have to just sit there patiently for a few moments with nothing to do during clearing up, but that can't be helped.

If you have no sink (poor you!). Try using three buckets:
* One with clean water to fill water pots
* One empty for dirty brushes and paint water
* One half full of water to soak palettes; better still use some kind of disposable palettes.

Keeping artwork

You might want to keep a few examples for school records or for your own future reference. These can be stored in large polythene window display books or in a home-made sugar paper display book.

You, or the art co-ordinator, might want evidence of coverage and progression for a number of reasons. A sample of artwork with a few notes attached about resources, planning, focus, etc can be valuable for future use. A glance at the artwork alone can be enough to remind you what you did and enable you to do it again at a later date.

If you want to be really organized, you could also keep labels from the display with the artwork and file it somewhere others could access it.

Izzy Merlin, Year 5

Starting points and ideas for themes, topics or inspiration

Before you start painting

Backgrounds

Before you start any artwork, some consideration should be given to the background. Children should not always work on white, or even plain, paper.

The surface they work on, be it paper, card or whatever, could be coloured, patterned or textured. This might be ready-made or prepared by the children themselves.

Backgrounds can be printed, children could roll inked rollers over them in different colours, they might have been ragged (printed with screwed-up rags dipped in paint), textured, or they might be wet or dampened. Paper could be screwed up and then smoothed out again before it is worked on, or even screwed up, ironed after a first layer of paint is applied and then painted again.

It is important for children to consider backgrounds as part of their paintings, not just the white bits behind their picture.

Children should be encouraged to consider their backgrounds from the onset. They need to think about what might be in them and what colours they might be, as part of their whole composition.

Discussion and observation

Painting from observation – from looking at and representing what exists, as opposed to painting abstract feelings and moods – is easier if children have the opportunity to study how something looks. Whether this is through the work or from first-hand experience depends on the subject matter.

Painting from imagination is quite difficult for older children, because they are usually striving for realism and realism is difficult if there is no opportunity to examine how something actually looks. If it is not possible for whatever reason to look at the real thing, then the Internet is an excellent resource. If you have an interactive whiteboard, open up the Google search engine and click on 'Images'. If you then type in whatever it is you want to look at, eg dragons, it will bring up an enormous selection of images for

you to select and enlarge on the screen. There is usually a 'see full size image' option to click on, which will make the image larger so that all the children can see it.

Children can be directed to look at the basic shape of the subject, the colour, the surface texture, where the light falls, the darkest and lightest areas, etc.

They should also be encouraged to look at their environment and be given opportunities to express their ideas, thoughts and feelings about it.

The more children observe, handle and discuss the things they are going to paint, the more detailed their work will be. Before starting painting, encourage discussion and questions about the nature of the task, the objectives and the skills involved.

Experiences and stimuli for paintings

* Responding to excursions and outings
* Interpreting music, poetry, stories and drama
* Studying nature and man-made objects in the everyday world
* Investigating art materials
* Interpreting personal experiences, feelings and moods

Starting-points and subject ideas

* Animals, fish, insects
* Plants: flowers, trees, grasses
* Interiors: views through windows/doors; family scenes
* Domestic objects, food and utensils, furniture, still life
* Buildings, past and present, doors, roofs, windows, bricks
* Landscapes, rural and urban
* Water: sea, lakes, rivers
* Disasters: volcanoes, floods, tidal waves, famine
* Portraits, self, individual, group, miniatures
* Fantasy: dragons, fairies, magic, mystery, witches, wizards, etc
* Dreams, nightmares
* The future: transport, clothes, homes
* Space: travel, planets, sun, moon, etc
* Toys, games, past and present
* Fire: candles, flames, etc

* Light, shade, shadows, contrast
* Reflection: in water, in glass, on curved surfaces
* Weather: storm, rain, sun, wind, heat, cold, snow, frost
* Seasons: characteristics and colours
* Camouflage in animals, insects, birds, fish, etc
* Multicultural life and culture
* Artefacts linked to topics, history, science, etc
* Transport: cars, lorries, motorbikes, wheels, aeroplanes, trains
* Underground, caves, minerals, creatures, mines, tunnels
* Myths and legends
* Entertainment: circus, theatre, dance, music, puppets, fairs
* Sports and games: clothing, equipment, stars, Olympics
* Machines: cogs, chains, tools, engines, fantasy
* Advertising: magazines, television, hoardings, packaging
* Growth: animal, human, plant, communities
* Industry: factories, workers, canals, chimneys
* Clothing: fashion, costumes, fabrics, hats, shoes, past and present
* Past cultures: Egypt, Greece, etc
* Celebrations: birthdays, weddings, parties
* Food, drink
* Patterns: natural and man-made

* Movement: animal, human, speed, clouds, wind
* Habitats: jungle, desert, under stones, Arctic, etc
* Families: animal, human, plants, objects
* Time: clocks, watches, ageing
* Decorative arts: ceramics, weaving, jewellery
* War: weapons, uniforms, tanks, flags

Points for children to consider

When we ask children to make paintings, we may underestimate how many decisions have to be made and how many choices there are to be made.

When making a painting, here are just some of the points children might have to consider:

* What will the content of the painting be?
* Will the painting have a particular mood or feeling?
* What resources are needed to support the content of the painting?
* What type of background is needed?
* Will the background be one colour or several?
* Is the background an important part of the composition or is it neutral?
* What surface is the painting to be on?
* Will the surface be wet/damp or dry?
* Thinking and planning the composition of the painting.
* Whether to make some kind of preliminary drawing or marks.
* Where is a good place to begin the painting?
* What brush(es) will be needed for different parts of the painting?
* Which colour to start with?
* How much paint needs to be mixed to get started?
* Is the paint mixed to the desired consistency?
* Does one area need to be dry before it is worked on, or worked next to?
* What will happen to the under-layer of paint, if it is painted over?
* How will special effects be created?
* How will the impression of fur/foliage/distance/warmth, etc be created?
* Is it better to put in small details later?
* Can a desired effect be achieved by using special brush marks?
* Will texture be used, in part or all over?
* How does the painting look from a distance?
* Does it 'read' (make sense to the viewer)?
* Does anything need changing to improve the painting?
* Does the painting need to be finished in one session?
* Is the painting finished?

William Taylor-Jones, Year 5

Basic skills

Chris Smith, Year 6

Introducing powder paint

Why powder paint?

Powder colour is by far the best choice for colour mixing because it gives children the best opportunity to control the process of mixing and changing colour. Dry colour cannot be used straight from the pot; water has to be added and this involves children with the process from the onset.

Success depends on children having been taught powder paint handling as a specific skill. If it is taught in a separate session when the focus is dealing with the medium rather than creating a painting, then children are only fighting one battle. It is worth spending time on this battle, because when the children have mastered the medium they will be better able to create the effects they want when they come to use the skill in a painting.

Having the right containers and setting out the 'painting station' in a user-friendly way makes a world of difference. Teachers often think that powder paint makes more mess and work than ready-mixed paint but it does not. Indeed, while dry powder does have its difficulties, if it is controlled through good classroom organization, it is less messy than ready-mixed paint and certainly less wasteful.

What is powder paint? An explanation that can be read to children

All paint consists of 'pigment' – that is, a colour – and some kind of binding agent which holds it together and makes it stick to the support (paper, canvas, etc).

In the case of powder paint, the pigment has not yet been mixed with a binding agent. That has to be done by the artist, who in this case is you. The binding agent is water. So, when you add water to powder paint, you are in fact mixing your own paint.

Organization of paint and equipment

For all colour mixing activities, only six colours are necessary. These colours are:
* Two reds – vermilion and crimson
* Two blues – brilliant blue (ultramarine) and cyan (sometimes known as sky blue; it is a turquoisey blue)
* Two yellows – brilliant yellow (egg yellow) and lemon yellow.

These can be stored in six plastic paint wells that fit into a small tray and can be placed on the table. The advantage is that you can remove or change the selection of colours if you want to. Black and white are also useful as they cannot be created by mixing.

The paint wells can be refilled from larger powder paint containers, and the easiest way to do this is to use the paint well like a scoop and dip it directly into the container. Only the most trustworthy of art monitors can be entrusted with this task!

Equipment needed for powder painting
* Newspaper
* Paper for artwork
* One set of paint wells between two children
* One water pot between two
* One palette between two
* Paint, water and palettes need to be positioned so that children do not have to reach across each other to get to them. This causes water and paint to land on their paintings when it shouldn't.
* A test paper for each child to try out colours and dab brush on
* A pencil, for writing the child's name on the back of work, if nothing else
* At least one brush per child, a selection of brushes of different sizes is better to give children the opportunity to exercise choice.

Key skills in handling powder paint
* Controlling the amount of water on the brush and in the palette
* Getting the consistency of the paint right
* Mixing up enough of the colour
* Adding enough pigment
* Re-mixing the colour when necessary
* Transferring powder to the palette on a brush.

These skills are covered in the powder paint handling lesson on page 26. Children need to revisit this activity at least once a year. Other skills will be covered in colour mixing lessons, such as adding a little of a colour at a time to change a colour/shade.

Tips about using palettes

This is really just common sense, but it is surprising how often children need to have this explained to them.

Things to remind the children about include:

* Remember you are sharing the palette; decide with your partner which areas on/in the palette you will each have.
* Don't use every part of your palette straight off. Use the space sensibly.
* Don't come up and wash your palette every five minutes – it is a waste of paint and a waste of time.
* If all your spaces are full, look to see if you can re-use one area again. For example, if you want a brown but there is no space free, then if you have a red mixed up, you can add green to it to make your brown – or, if there is a green mixed up, you can add red to that to get brown. Similarly, if you want a purple and you have a blue mixed, then add red to it, and so on. You don't necessarily need to mix the colour from scratch.
* If you do wash your palette, dry it thoroughly or the excess water will make all your new colours too watery.
* Washed palettes are better dried with a damp J-cloth than a paper towel. Paper towels are not absorbent enough for the job, and anyway it is a waste of paper.
* When you wash your palette, don't turn the water on full blast and hold the palette under it or you will be sprayed with water. Always angle the palette so that the dirty water runs down into the sink, not down you, nor the person next to you (although saying this may give them ideas!)

There are other important skills when painting, but these apply to many different painting media, not just powder paint: for example, knowing when to change the water; looking after the brushes. Those aspects will need reinforcing at the beginning of most painting lessons.

Pitfalls of powder paint

* It is difficult for children to mix a large amount of a colour. If they need a lot of paint, perhaps for a group or large-scale activity, then ready-mixed paint is more appropriate.
* It is hard to re-mix the same colour when it has run out and it will run out quickly. Children need to try to remember how they mixed their colour so that they can achieve that shade again, particularly with browns.
* Children will need to be careful transferring paint to the palette from the paint wells. They tend to try to balance precarious heaps of dry powder on their brushes that can be knocked, and then will sprinkle powder everywhere. The excess powder paint will also change the colour too drastically. They need to be reminded that it is best to change a shade or colour gradually with small amounts at a time.
* If you are mixing a lot of paint, the powder can tend to float on the surface of the water and be tricky to mix in. This is particularly true of black and of the metallic powder paints. A drop of washing-up liquid in the water solves this.
* The colours look lovely and bright when just painted, but they lose a little of this brightness when dry.

Tom Worsley, Year 5

KEY SKILL Investigating paintbrushes and brush strokes

Year 5 pupil

<table>
<tr><td>

Time
1 hour

Resources
Newspaper to cover tables

Per group of 5 or 6 children:
Piles of brushes in as many different sizes, shaped ends and lengths of handle as you have in school
2 or 3 paint colours (could be any paint except watercolours)
2 water pots
1 palette

For each child:
A3 piece of paper

For the teacher:
One of each type of brush to show
A2 piece of paper to demonstrate the brush marks
Something to fix paper to board
Brush information on page 12

National Curriculum
2a, 4a

</td></tr>
</table>

Introduction

Artists use many different types of brushes, depending on what kind of paint they are using, how big or how small the painting is and what kind of effect they want to make. Today you will be looking at the different types of paintbrush and making as many different marks as you can with each type.

Practical activity

* Put a big pile of different brushes in front of each group of children and ask them to sort them into piles according to size, handle and end shapes.
* Point out that the ends of the brushes may be different lengths and different shapes, and can be made of different kinds of hair.
* Ask the children to look for any indication on the brush handles as to the size.
* When the brushes have been sorted, explain that different brushes are used for different purposes and will make different marks.
* Explain that the metal part of the brush is called the ferrule and that the bristles/hair can be made from different materials, some natural and some man-made (see brush information on page 12).
* Tell the children that they should hold the brushes as they would hold a pencil. The best place to hold a brush is just above where the ferrule meets the handle (see Potential pitfall below).
* Ask them to mix a slightly thinned solution of paint, then take a short-handled, small soft brush and paint some straight lines and some wavy lines on the paper. Now ask them to repeat this, but press down the brush a little so the lines are wider. Demonstrate.
* They could try painting tiny dots, big blobs, flicks and brush strokes of different lengths and thicknesses. Demonstrate.
* Encourage them to make as many different marks as they can.
* They should now repeat the process with different sizes and types of brush; they could record the size and type of the brush.

Potential pitfall

Children often hold the brush handles either very close to the bristles and get paint all over their fingers which then transfers itself to the painting, or they hold them too far down the handle which makes it difficult for them to control the brush.

Using different brush strokes in a painting

USING SKILL

Time
30 min

Resources
Newspaper to cover tables

Per group of 5 or 6 children:
2 or 3 paint colours (could be any paint except watercolours)
Collection of brushes of different types and different sizes
2 water pots
2 palettes

For each child:
A4 piece of black paper

For the teacher:
One of each type of brush to show
A2 piece of paper to demonstrate the brush marks
Something to fix paper to board

National Curriculum
2a, 4a, 5a

Joss Warren, Year 5 (fields and hedges)

Introduction
You have tried out making marks with different sizes and kinds of brush, and now you can paint a picture using those brushes. It doesn't matter what you paint (or the subject might be topic led), but what does matter is that you try to make as many different brush strokes and use as many different types and sizes of brush as you can.

Practical activity
* Go over the types, shapes and sizes of brushes if necessary (brush information is on page 12).
* Ask the children to take note of the number on the brush handles which shows the size, and also to notice the different sizes and types and shapes of the bristles.
* Remind the children to hold the brushes as they would hold a pencil. The best place to hold a brush is just above where the metal bit (the ferrule) meets the handle. However, they could try holding the brush at the end of the handle, halfway down, and with their arm fully extended (if they are working on an easel), to see what difference it makes and which they prefer.

* Go over the different brush strokes they could make. Demonstrate tiny dots, long lines, thick lines, thin lines, zigzags, big blobs and brush strokes of different lengths and thicknesses.
* Extend this by telling them that they can work quickly or slowly, use the brush in different directions, press hard or gently, use the top, side or edge of the brush, or roll or splay the bristles. Demonstrate.
* Encourage them to make as many different marks as they can in their paintings.

Care of brushes
Explain to the children that:
* Brushes should always be washed at the end of a session.
* Watercolour brushes or very dirty brushes can be washed in warm soapy water.
* The ends of watercolour brushes should be shaped back into a point with the fingers after washing.
* Never leave watercolour or soft-bristled brushes ends down in the water pot when not in use. Lay them flat on the table.
* Brushes should always be stored handle-end downward or flat in a tray, never bristles downward.

KEY SKILL | Powder paint handling

Time
30 min
Resources
Newspaper
Full set of powder paint colours:
• 2 reds
• 2 blues
• 2 yellows and black (see page 22)
Water pots
Palettes
Medium long-handled brushes
Cartridge paper
Sketchbooks
Test papers
National Curriculum
2a, 4a

Year 5 pupil trying out strong colours

Introduction

Today you are going to be learning (or revisiting) how to handle powder paint. We will be practising how to mix the paint to the right consistency, how to use your palettes, when to change your water and how to get the best out of the colours.

Practical activity

※ The lesson could be started by reading the information about powder paint at the start of this chapter (page 22).

※ Explain that when the children are mixing up paint it is better not to use a delicate brush. They should use a medium, long-handled brush.

※ Remind them to hold the brush just above the ferrule (metal bit).

※ Demonstrate the following procedure:
1. Dip the brush in the water.
2. Stroke the brush on the top of the water pot to remove surplus water.
3. Dip the wet brush into powder colour and transfer to the mixing palette.
4. Stir the brush around until the powder and water are blended.
5. Repeat the process until enough paint is mixed for the children's needs.
6. Test the colour on test paper with just a few dabs or lines of paint.

※ Explain that too much water makes the paint very thin and runny and that the consistency should be like cream rather than milk. If the colour is mixed to the creamy consistency then the colour will be as bright and strong as it will go – the crimson will be a deep strong crimson, the cyan will be a deep strong cyan, and so on; the colour will show its full 'value'.

※ Ask the children to experiment with the consistency of the paint and to see how strong they can make a colour.

※ Tell the children that if they can see the bottom of the palette through the paint then they have not mixed up enough to paint a strong colour, so they should add more powdered colour to it.

※ Suggest children repeat this process with all six of the colours and then black.

※ Next mix an orange, a green and a purple. Tell the children to do this by adding powder paint into an existing mixed colour in their palette, rather than by using a new area of the palette. For example, if they want orange, add a red to a yellow or a yellow to a red. This is good practice for future painting sessions and will reduce the queue at the sink to wash palettes.

※ Explain that they should wash their brushes between colours, always wiping the brush on the top edge of the water pot afterwards to control the amount of water going into the paint mixture.

※ Water should be changed when it is dirty. Tell the children that they can test if the water needs changing by putting a cleaned brush in the water and dabbing a few watery marks on their test paper. If the dabs are not coloured, then the water doesn't need changing.

Naming paint colours

SKILL

Francis Zoat, Year 5

Time
20 min

Resources
Newspaper to cover tables

Per pair of children:
6 powder paint or ready-mixed colours:
- 2 reds: vermilion and crimson
- 2 blues: brilliant blue and cyan
- 2 yellows: brilliant and lemon yellow
1 water pot
1 palette

For each child:
1 medium long-handled brush
Sketchbooks

For the teacher:
An A2 piece of paper to demonstrate the colours
Masking tape
Colour wheel from page 53 to show

National Curriculum
2a, 4a

Introduction

As you know, paint colours have names, and we are going to go over the colours and their names and their characteristics. This knowledge will be useful to you whenever you are colour mixing. You will be recording the colours and their names in your sketchbooks so you can look them up if you need to do so another time. When artists go into an art shop to buy a colour, they will say exactly which colour they want by name, as there are many different shades of every colour. There are two blues, two reds and two yellows in front of you. Does anyone remember any of the names of the six colours?

Practical activity

✳ Suggest that the children look first at the two yellows and notice the difference. Ask them how they would describe the yellows and in what way they are different. You could tell them that the brilliant yellow is slightly darker and a little closer to orange on the colour wheel, while the lemon yellow is paler and nearer to green. You could also show them the colour wheel on page 53.

✳ Tell them the darker yellow is called 'Brilliant Yellow' and that it is a bit like the colour of an egg yolk.

1. Ask the children to paint a patch of brilliant yellow in their sketchbooks and label it 'Brilliant Yellow'.

2. Demonstrate by painting a patch of brilliant yellow paint on the large piece of paper and writing 'Brilliant Yellow' next to it. Tape the paper to the board with masking tape.

✳ Explain that the other lighter yellow is called 'Lemon Yellow'.

✳ Repeat steps 1 and 2 above but using lemon yellow.

✳ Explain that the deeper red is called 'Crimson' and the lighter more orange-red is called 'Vermilion'. Ask the children to notice the difference between the two colours. Explain that crimson has a touch of blue in it and so is nearer to purple on the colour wheel, while vermilion has a touch of yellow and so is nearer to orange.

✳ Repeat steps 1 and 2 above but using each of the two reds.

✳ Explain that the darker blue is called 'Brilliant Blue' and the lighter blue is called 'Cyan'. Cyan has a touch of yellow and so is nearer to green on the colour wheel, while brilliant blue has a touch of red and so is closer to purple.

✳ Repeat steps 1 and 2 above but using both blues.

✳ Run over the names of the colours at the end of the session. The children will need reminding of these colour names almost every time they paint. It seems to take a long time to sink in, perhaps because they do not use these names in any other context.

27

Painting a picture in powder paint

USING SKILL

Time
1 hour

Resources
Newspaper
Full set of powder paint colours:
• 2 reds
• 2 blues
• 2 yellows and black – see page 22
Water pots
Palettes
Medium long-handled brushes
Fine brushes
Cartridge paper
Test papers
Access to Picasso's painting 'Weeping Woman' (1937)
Information about Picasso (pages 101–102)

National Curriculum
2a, 4a,c, 5a

Rob Steel, Year 6

Introduction

You have been developing your skills in handling powder paint and painting in strong colours. Today you are going to try to use those skills in a painting.

Show the children the painting and say: 'In this painting, Picasso has used colours and shapes in a dramatic way to help communicate the woman's anguish. The jagged black lines are like broken glass, and the bared teeth and the teardrops all help to make a powerful and harrowing image. You are going to paint a face, showing a powerful emotion like fear, rage or grief, using colour and shape to help communicate those feelings.'

Practical activity

❋ Study and discuss the painting with the class and ask children why and how this painting works so well.
❋ Suggest that the children then draw the outline of a face very lightly, just to make sure they can fit it on the page.
❋ Next, they should divide the face into a few angular shapes, and add eyes, mouth and hair. They could include a nose and a hat if they want, but they should not have too much detail as this should be a simple, dramatic picture.
❋ Suggest they consider the background and think about how the colours and shapes could add to the mood of the picture.
❋ Once a simple outline is marked out, the children should consider the colours. They could use complementary colours (see page 54) to increase the dramatic impact.
❋ Remind the children of steps 1–6 from the powder paint handling lesson on page 26.
❋ Ask them to paint in the face and background shapes, and to aim to paint the colours as strong as they will go, giving them their full 'value'.
❋ When the paint is dry, the shapes could be outlined in black paint and lines added to increase the drama of the picture.

Making a colour lighter without using white: changing tone in colour (method 1)

KEY SKILL

Time
20 min

Resources
Newspaper to cover tables

Per pair of children:
Powder paint or ready-mixed colours
1 pot of brilliant blue or crimson
1 water pot
1 palette

For each child:
1 fine long-handled brush
Sketchbooks or cartridge paper
Copy of resource sheet 5, page 124,
if needed
Test paper

For the teacher:
An A2 piece of paper to demonstrate
the colours
Masking tape to fix it to the board

National Curriculum
2a, 4a

Year 6 pupil (using resource sheet 5, page 124)

Introduction

Every colour has its own full value, that is to say the colour it will go when it is mixed to its strongest and painted with the least amount of water. Colours can always be made lighter by adding white, but this can make the colour seem a bit chalky or dull. The way to make a colour a lighter tone without using white, is to use more water and less paint (pigment). This allows the white of the paper to shine through the paint and it is this that gives it its lightness. The colour becomes 'translucent', which literally means the light (or lightness of the paper) travels through it. Today you are going to practise making a colour lighter without using white paint, and later on you will use this skill in a painting.

Practical activity

※ Ask the children to mix up whichever colour has been chosen for this exercise. For the purposes of this lesson, we will assume this is brilliant blue, because this is a colour which, when given its full value, has a deep tone and so gives good scope for creating a range of tones. Crimson is also a good choice.

※ If they are using powder paint, remind the children that the paint needs to be at least the consistency of cream if it is to have its full value.

※ Next, the children should make a dab of paint on the test paper to check the blue is a strong and deep as it will go. Demonstrate just how strong the colour can be.

※ Now tell them to paint a patch on their paper of the strongest, deepest tone of brilliant blue (the full value of the colour).

※ Next, ask them to experiment on their test papers to see what happens if they use a little less pigment (powder or ready-mixed pure colour) and a little more water. Explain that they control the proportion of pigment to water to vary the tone.

※ Point out that they will need to control the amount of water so that the paint is a light tone but not too runny. This might require some practice and a demonstration.

※ Once they have experimented, challenge them to create a collection of dabs of paint ranging from deepest to palest brilliant blue.

Making a colour lighter without using white: dragging the colour (method 2)

Time
15 min

Resources
1 powder paint or ready-mixed colour:
• blue or red
1 water pot
1 palette
Sketchbooks or A4 cartridge paper

For each child:
1 long-handled brush for mixing
Test paper

For the teacher:
An A2 piece of paper to demonstrate
Masking tape to fix it to the board

National Curriculum
2a, 4a

Year 5 pupil

Introduction

You are going to try making a colour lighter by dragging the paint along the paper with a clean wet brush. This is a very useful technique and one that you will be able to use in your paintings. Adding white to a colour will make it lighter, but sometimes it can make the colour seem a little dull and chalky. With this technique, it is the white of the paper shining through that makes the lightness. It is a technique that can be applied to many different types of paint and it is particularly important in watercolours.

Practical activity

❋ Ask the children to mix up a colour as bright and as strong as it will go (to its full value).
❋ Tell them to test the colour on the test paper to check that it is a deep tone.
❋ Explain to the children that a variation of tones can be achieved in a continuous flow from dark to light in this sequence:
   1. Paint a patch of full value blue or red.
   2. Wash the brush so that it is clean and wet.

   3. Place the clean wet brush on the edge of the painted patch before it dries.
   4. Drag/pull the colour away from the patch, creating a mid-tone.
   5. Continue for a few centimetres.
   6. Wash the brush again.
   7. Place the clean wet brush over the last bit of paint painted and drag the colour along a bit further.
❋ Repeat steps 6 and 7 until there is no colour left.
❋ Explain that this technique can be used for a long area of tone change, as they have done just now, or over a shorter distance. It can also be used for a small tone change, such as from a mid-tone to a light tone.

Using the technique of dragging the colour to make a colour lighter

Time
1 hour

Resources
Newspaper to cover tables
Set out on a separate table:
A few old toothbrushes or old
washing-up brushes
Some white ready-mixed paint

Per pair of children:
Powder paint or ready-mixed colours:
• 2 blues: brilliant blue and cyan
1 water pot
1 palette

For each child:
1 long-handled brush for mixing
1 medium fine short-handled brush
Test paper

For the teacher:
An A2 piece of paper to demonstrate
Masking tape to fix it to the board

National Curriculum
2a, 4a

Laura Gray, Year 6

Note

This lesson can be applied to any colours and any appropriate subjects, eg sunsets for reds or jungles for greens. It is suggested that colours are limited so that the focus is on the controlling of the tone rather than on colour mixing.

Introduction

You have been practising making colours lighter by dragging the paint with a wet brush. Now you are going to paint a seascape (or whatever) using that skill. You should use a wide range of tones of blue from deepest to lightest blue.

Practical activity

※ Ask children to mix up a little brilliant blue in the palest tone, and to paint a line two-thirds of the way up the paper to represent the horizon.

※ Next, using their long-handled brushes, they should mix up some brilliant blue to its deepest tone and test it on their test papers.

※ Tell the children to use their finer brushes to paint some wavy lines across the lower two-thirds of the paper to represent waves. These should be in deepest brilliant blue.

※ Next, the children should add a little water to the brilliant blue mix to create a lighter tone of blue, test the colour on a test paper to check it is a little lighter and then paint along under the lower edge of the waves, creating a slightly lighter wavy blue line.

※ Now tell the children to drag the colour down from each wave using the method covered in the previous lesson.

※ Next, clouds can be outlined in a very pale blue and the sky can be painted, starting at the top with a deep tone of blue and then dragging the colour down with a wet brush in the same way as before, leaving the clouds white.

※ When the painting is finished (it does not need to be dry), the children can spatter white paint lightly over the picture, using an old toothbrush dipped in white paint, to create the effect of spray. Information about spattering paint is on page 107.

Colour mixing

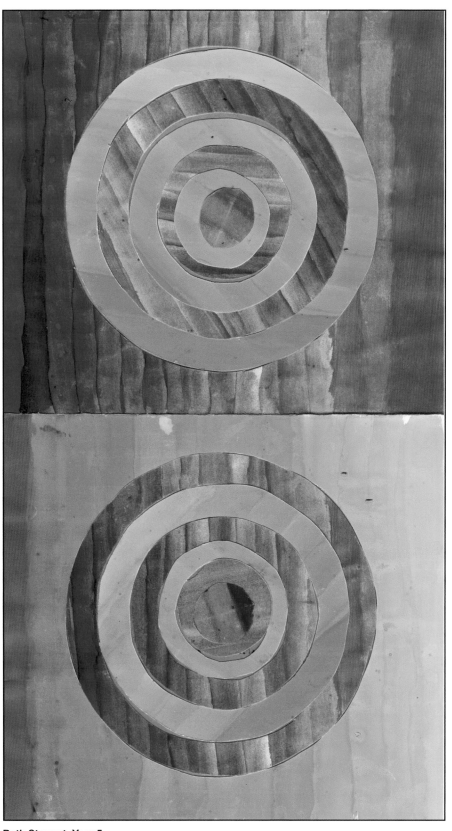

Beth Stewart, Year 5

Mixing colours

Crucial to the teaching of painting is recognition that the careful matching, mixing and application of colour requires time.

Mixing and using paint needs much time for the preparation and for introductory activities – so much so that at the end of the allotted time, there may be little to show other than a mass of apparently meaningless splodges of colour and marks. However, the time spent on such activities is never wasted. It provides children with invaluable information to store in their visual memory, so that when they are engaged in a painting activity they have some reference on which to draw.

Colour mixing is one of the most significant aspects in learning how to use paint, and it invites children to discriminate between myriad qualities of shade and tint. Suddenly their paintings will come alive as this full range of colour is at their disposal.

The skill of mixing paint will require development over a number of years. There is so much to learn, and each stage needs to be carefully developed and built on in the future.

Children's descriptive language of colour can be developed side by side with the skills of colour mixing, and they should be encouraged to have a personal response to colour and to become able to relate it to mood and atmosphere.

If colour mixing is not being prioritized, the many liquid ready-mixed paints that are now on the market are an easy-to-use alternative to powder paint, though it is worth pointing out that these liquid paints may comprise only basic powder colours mixed with water and a thickener. When their cost is considered, this might make them seem an expensive convenience.

Even when using ready-mixed colours, it is still important to encourage colour mixing. To always provide a brush in each pot of ready-mixed colour is to deny pupils a learning opportunity.

Paint provides the best and most flexible medium for exploring colour. For general painting, powder paints give children the best opportunity to do this effectively – but ultimately this is a matter of personal choice by the teacher, and the principles of colour mixing will hold good for all types of paint.

Colour mixing and exploration in acrylics, oils and watercolours are covered in chapters specific to these media later in this book.

Mixing their own colours will help children to develop an awareness and appreciation of colour, and that is a life-enhancing ability which should not be undervalued.

Hopefully, by the end of Key Stage 2, pupils will be able to confidently select a range of colours most appropriate for the subject matter and task in hand.

Colour mixing tips
* Crimson is the best red for mixing purples.
* Vermilion is the best red for mixing oranges.
* Cyan and lemon yellow make vivid greens.
* Brilliant blue (ultramarine) and brilliant yellow make natural greens.
* Black and yellow make olive greens.

Black:
* Brilliant blue, crimson, vermilion and brilliant yellow make a near black.
* A pure black cannot be mixed.
* Black added to colours darkens colours but also dulls them.

White:
* White lightens colours but can also dull them.
* Touches of other colours added to white will make different types of white.

Brown:
* Different combinations of the three primaries make different browns.
* Green and red make brown.
* Vermilion and blue make a kind of brown.
* Yellow and purple make a grey/brown.

Skin tones: (all need slight adjustments to match)
* A little of crimson or vermilion with a lot of white and a touch of yellow and the teeniest touch of blue will make a pale skin tone.
* Warm brown and some white make a darker skin tone. Small touches of other colours will vary the shade.
* Cream can be made with white and brilliant yellow and a touch of red.
* Crimson and white make good pinks but not good skin tones.

Note: Colour mixing with watercolour colours and oils are covered on pages 74 and 88, respectively, because some of the watercolour and oil colours have different names and also there is an extended range of colours to work with.

Recording colour mixing

 SKILL

Time
45 min

Resources
Newspaper to cover tables

Per pair of children:
Powder paint or ready-mixed colours:
• crimson + brilliant blue
• cyan + lemon yellow
• brilliant yellow + vermilion
1 water pot
1 palette

For each child:
1 medium long-handled brush
A4 cartridge paper or sketchbook
A pencil
Test paper

For the teacher:
A3 piece of paper to demonstrate the
process, and tape to stick it up

National Curriculum
2a, 4a

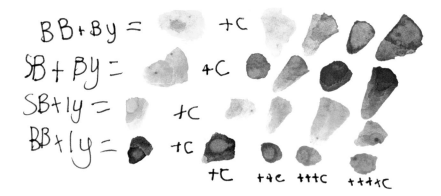

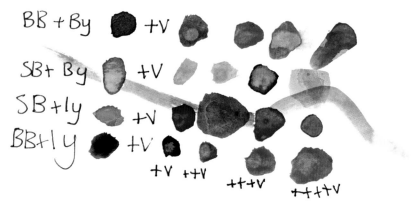

Year 6 pupil

Introduction

*Today you are going to mix your own colours and record how
you made the colours so you could make them again. It is
possible to buy books which show how to make new colours
by using different combinations of paint colours. Artists use
these, as there are almost limitless possibilities when mixing
colours, so it can be very difficult to remember them. Often
artists will make their own record of colour mixing for future
reference, and that is what you will be doing.*

Practical activity

❋ Tell children that they will need to devise
a system and a code for recording colour
mixing that will help them to remember which
combinations they have already tried and will
make it easy to re-make the colour another
time.
❋ Suggest that they create a letter code for
each of the six colours, eg BB for Brilliant
Blue, CB for Cyan Blue (so as not to confuse
it will C for Crimson – or cyan could be
renamed as 'Sky Blue' for this exercise).
This code could be written on the board and
children could copy it into their sketchbooks.

❋ Suggest they start with one colour and add
another to it. For example, they could make
a green with brilliant blue and brilliant yellow,
write: BB + BY and then paint a dot of that
green. Demonstrate this.
❋ Next, they could add a little crimson to that
green and label it BB + BY + C
❋ They could add a little more crimson to the
new colour and label it BB + BY + C + C and
so on. More able children will quickly devise
their own system, while others made need
more support and suggestions.
❋ The children could try to recreate their new
colours another time, perhaps in the context
of a painting (see the lesson on page 52).
❋ Colour recording should be kept for future
reference. If the work has not been done in
sketchbooks, then it should be stuck in so
that the children can refer back to it.

Working in two blues

SKILL

Time
45 min

Resources
Newspaper to cover tables

Per pair of children:
Powder paint or ready-mixed colours:
- 2 reds: vermilion and crimson
- 2 blues: brilliant blue and cyan
- 2 yellows: brilliant and lemon yellow
1 water pot
1 palette

For each child:
1 medium long-handled brush for mixing
1 fine brush
Sketchbooks

For the teacher:
Colour wheel on page 53 to show

National Curriculum
2a, 4a,b, 5b

Archie Muirhead, Year 5

Introduction
You know the names of the paint colours. We are going to paint in just blue today. You can try to vary those blues slightly by adding a little of other colours to make different blues, and then try to paint a picture using only blue.

Practical activity
- Suggest that the children look at just the two blues and take note of the difference. Ask them how they would describe the blues and in what way they are different. You could tell them that the brilliant blue is slightly darker and a little nearer to purple on the spectrum, while cyan is lighter and nearer to green. You could also show them the colour wheel on page 53.
- Ask if they can remember the names of the two blues. They could check in their sketchbooks from the previous lesson.

- Tell them to try adding a little of other colours to each blue in turn and to label each new shade as they do so. They could use a code like BB for brilliant blue, C for Crimson, CB for Cyan Blue, etc.
- Then they could paint a miniature in their blues – a small portrait, a seascape or whatever they think is appropriate to the blues they are using.
- This activity could be done with the reds, but not so easily with the yellows as yellow changes very quickly into green or orange.
- Run over the names of the colours at the end of the session. Children will need reminding of these colour names almost every time they paint. It seems to take a long time to sink in, perhaps because they do not use these names in any other context.

Mixing and recording colours: browns

SKILL

Time
45 min

Resources
Newspaper to cover tables

Per pair of children:
Powder paint or ready-mixed colours:
- 2 reds: vermilion and crimson
- 2 blues: brilliant blue and cyan
- 2 yellows: brilliant and lemon yellow
1 water pot
1 palette

For each child:
1 medium long-handled brush
A4 cartridge paper or sketchbook
A pencil
Test paper

For the teacher:
A3 piece of paper to demonstrate their process and tape to stick it up

National Curriculum
2a, 4a

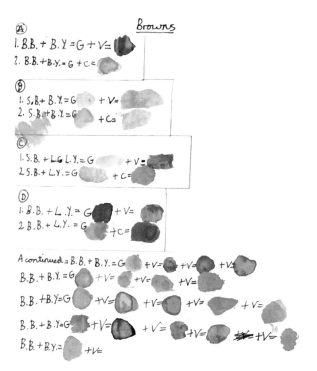

Year 6 pupil

Introduction
Today you are going to mix different browns and record how you make the browns so that you could make them again. Browns are 'tertiary colours' and they are made by mixing the three primaries together in different combinations and proportions. The usual answer to the question, 'How do you make brown?' would be, 'By mixing red and green.' This is correct, but since green is made by mixing two primaries (blue and yellow), it comes to the same thing. Different blues and reds and yellows combined make different browns, and you are going to investigate and record this.

Practical activity
❊ This exercise could be organized in different ways, eg different groups of children could investigate different combinations of colours.
❊ Combinations are:
  - Vermilion, lemon yellow and cyan
  - Vermilion, brilliant yellow and cyan
  - Vermilion, brilliant yellow and brilliant blue
  - Vermilion, lemon yellow and brilliant blue
  - Crimson, lemon yellow and cyan
  - Crimson, lemon yellow and brilliant blue
  - Crimson, brilliant yellow and cyan
  - Crimson, brilliant yellow and brilliant blue

❊ Some combinations will make yellow-browns like ochre, while some will make khaki-browns and some rusty browns.
❊ Tell the children that they will need to devise a system and a code for recording colour mixing that will help them to remember which combinations they have already tried, and to make it easy to re-make the colour another time.
❊ For example, vermilion, lemon yellow and cyan blue would be: V + LY + CB.
❊ Suggest that they create a letter code for each of the six colours, eg BB for Brilliant Blue, CB for Cyan Blue (so as not to confuse it will C for Crimson – or cyan could be renamed as 'Sky Blue' for this exercise). This code could be written on the board and children could copy it into their sketchbooks.
❊ Explain that different proportions of the colours will give them different browns. For example, if they are investigating combination no. 1, one dab of vermilion, one dab of lemon and two dabs of cyan will make a different brown than if they have more vermilion and less cyan, and so on.
❊ Tell the children to record their mixing, using their code, as they go along.
❊ Point out that every brown they make can also be made a lighter or darker tone by using more or less water. The range is enormous.

USING SKILL

Mixing and painting in browns

Time
45 min

Resources
Newspaper to cover tables
String
PVA glue
Thick glue brushes

Per pair of children:
Powder paint or ready-mixed colours:
- 2 reds: vermilion and crimson
- 2 blues: brilliant blue and cyan
- 2 yellows: brilliant and lemon yellow
1 water pot
1 palette
1 pair of scissors

For each child:
1 medium long-handled brush
A3 cartridge paper
Previous brown mix recordings
A pencil
Test paper
A few stones (with at least one flat side)

National Curriculum
2a, 4a, 5a

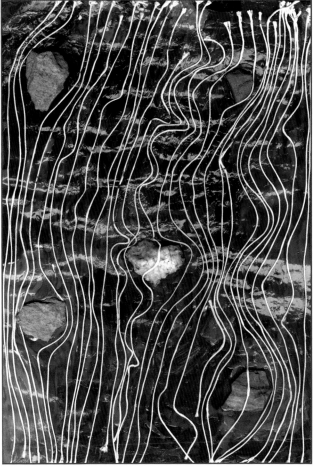

Danny Hudson, Year 6

Note

In this example, the children painted the stones beneath a stream as they were doing a study of rivers, but your pupils might prefer to choose their own subjects. They will need something that will give them plenty of scope to use as many different browns as possible, eg mud wrestlers, an autumn scene or a camouflaged brown animal.

Introduction

You are going to re-mix some of those browns you made in the last lesson and paint a picture using them. Look back at your brown mixing recordings and remind yourself of all the different colours that you made. Try to use as many different browns as you can in your painting, and to leave very little background paper showing.

Practical activity

※ Tell children to cover the paper with patches of different browns to represent the stones or autumn leaves at the bottom of a stream, and remind them that in nature two things are rarely exactly the same colour.

※ While the paint is drying, tell them to cut a number of lengths of string, several centimetres longer than the length of the paintings. 31 pieces of string have been used in this painting!

※ If the paintings are still not dry, children could draw a few stone shapes in their sketchbooks, and then a series of wavy lines to represent the movement of water around stones as it rushes down the river.

※ Once the paintings are dry, tell the children to paint a thick coat of PVA glue over them and stick on a few stones, flat side downwards, or they may fall off.

※ While the glue is still wet, tell them to lay their string down lengthways along the painting, starting at the edge. Each successive piece of string should follow and slightly distort the line of the previous piece of string.

※ Where a piece of string meets a stone, the string could go over or around it, as water would.

Mixing secondary colours

KEY SKILL

Time
2 hours

Resources
Newspaper to cover tables

Per pair of children:
Powder paint or ready-mixed colours:
• crimson + vermilion
• cyan + brilliant blue
• brilliant yellow + lemon yellow
1 water pot
1 palette

For each child:
1 medium long-handled brush
A4 cartridge paper or sketchbook
Test paper

For the teacher:
A3 piece of paper to demonstrate the
colours, and tape to stick it up

National Curriculum
2a, 4a

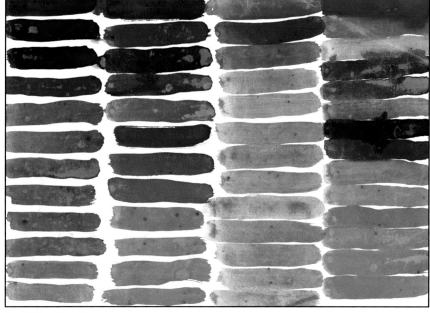

Zoe Elder, Year 5

Introduction
*Today we are going to mix the three secondary colours, but
we are going to do this in a systematic way, making sure we
try all the combinations.*

Practical activity
* Revise what primary and secondary colours
  are (page 54).
* Ask the children which two primary colours
  are mixed together to make orange, green
  and purple.
* Explain that any yellow and any blue will
  make a green, but that different blues and
  different yellows will produce different greens;
  also, different proportions of blue and yellow
  will produce different greens.
* Tell them that cyan and brilliant yellow will
  produce green, but a lot of cyan and a little
  brilliant yellow will make a deep green while
  a little cyan and a lot of brilliant yellow will
  make a light green. Say that this applies to all
  the blue/yellow combinations, which are:
  • cyan + brilliant yellow
  • cyan + lemon yellow
  • brilliant blue + brilliant yellow
  • brilliant blue + lemon yellow

* Explain that in order to make sure they try
  out all the combinations, they will need to
  be systematic. They could devise their own
  system or use the one explained below and
  illustrated above.
* Tell them to fold the paper to make four
  columns.
* Next, mix up a blue and paint a line across
  the top of one of the columns. Label the blue.
* Now add a little of one of the yellows, test the
  colour on the test paper to make sure there has
  been a slight change in colour and then paint a
  line beneath the first. Demonstrate if necessary.
* Continue in this way down the paper, always
  testing the colour on the test paper before
  painting with it and adjusting it if necessary,
  until the pure yellow is reached – and then
  label that.
* Repeat this for the other three blue/yellow
  combinations, and then mix the oranges and
  purples.
* The work can be stuck into sketchbooks, or
  work can be done directly in their sketchbooks
  in the first place. They will be able to look
  back and see how they made the different
  secondary colours and recreate them.

Teacher tip
Always add the lighter colour into the darker, eg
add yellow into the blue, rather than blue into
yellow. If blue is added into yellow, the yellow
changes too quickly into a strong green and it is
difficult to control the colour change.

Painting in secondary colours

Time
1 hour
Resources
Newspaper to cover tables
Per pair of children:
6 powder paint or ready-mixed
colours:
• 2 reds: vermilion and crimson
• 2 blues: brilliant blue and cyan
• 2 yellows: brilliant and lemon yellow
1 water pot
1 palette
For each child:
Their colour mixing work from the
lesson on page 38 for reference
A choice of brush sizes
Test paper
Cartridge paper
National Curriculum
2a, 4a, 5a

Daisy Waldron, Year 5

Introduction
You have learned how to mix a wide range of secondary colours – not just one orange using one red and one yellow, but many oranges using combinations of different reds and different yellows. You did the same with greens and purples, and now is your chance to use as many of those colours as you can in a painting.

Practical activity
※ Discuss with children suitable subjects for each of the secondary colours, and the ideas generated could be put on the board. The colours do not need to all be in oranges, greens or purples, but should be predominantly in one of those colours.
※ Possible subjects could be:
  • Oranges: sunsets, fires, volcanic eruptions, autumn leaves or still lifes with flowers and fruit.
  • Greens: jungles, forests, gardens, hedges, monsters, or still lifes with foliage, glass bottles and fruit.
  • Purples: moorland, flowers, unusual skies, royal costumes, fantastical creatures, eg purple people eater, dragons or wizards.
※ When the children have chosen their colour and subject, suggest they draw the composition roughly in a diluted version of their colour, dark enough to be able to see but light enough to change.
※ Remind them of the range of colours possible by using combinations of different reds, yellows and blues.
※ Suggest they look at their collections of oranges, greens and purples from the secondary colour mixing lesson.
※ Explain that they could use the deeper-toned colours as shadows, which are rarely truly black anyway.

Changing one colour into another

SKILL

Andrew Newton, Year 6

Time
45 min

Resources
Newspaper to cover tables

Per pair of children:
Powder paint or ready-mixed colours:
- crimson + vermilion
- cyan + brilliant blue
- brilliant yellow + lemon yellow
1 water pot
1 palette

For each child for the picture:
1 medium long-handled brush
Glue stick
Square of cartridge paper
Craft knife
Test paper
Background paper

For the teacher:
A3 piece of paper to demonstrate the process, and tape to stick it up

National Curriculum
2a, 4a

Introduction
Today you are going to change one colour into another by gradually adding small amounts of paint at a time and controlling the colour change.

Practical activity
* Ask children to decide which colour they would like to change into which. Here, brilliant blue has been changed into vermilion and then vermilion has been changed into brilliant yellow.
* Tell them to mix up plenty of their darker colour in their palettes, then test it on their test papers to make sure it is as strong as it will go.
* Next, they should paint a stripe of their chosen pure colour across the paper from one side to the other.
* Tell them to add a little of their chosen second colour (the one they want to turn the first one into) to their first colour.
* Next, they should test it on their test paper to make sure it is just a little different, and then paint a stripe of this colour immediately under the first stripe, leaving no white paper

between the two colours.
* The children should now add a little more of the second colour to the mixture they have just made, test the colour to make sure it is just a little different (not too different), and then paint another stripe of this colour beneath the last.
* They should continue in this way until they have changed their first colour into their second. (Potential pitfall: If the first colour runs out, the children will need to re-mix it and then add the appropriate amount of the second colour to get back to where they were.)
* If they have not reached the bottom of the paper yet, they could now continue to change the new colour into a third colour, as in this example.
* To make the picture above, children should:
  - Draw a circle on the other side (draw around something).
  - An adult then cuts the circle out with craft knife.
  - The children stick the background down on another piece of paper.
  - Then they put the circle back in the middle and turn it so that the colours are in a different position.
  - Glue it down. This image fits in well with a space topic.

Changing and blending colours by adding a little paint at a time

SKILL

Time
45 min

Resources
Newspaper to cover tables

Per pair of children:
Powder paint or ready-mixed colours:
- 2 reds: vermilion and crimson
- 2 blues: brilliant blue and cyan
- 2 yellows: brilliant and lemon yellow
1 water pot and 1 palette

For each child:
1 medium long-handled brush
A4 cartridge paper
Test papers

For teacher:
A2 paper to demonstrate and tape to fix to the board

National Curriculum
2a, 4a,b

Tom Murphy, Year 6

Introduction
Today you are going to learn a very useful painting skill, one that most painters have to master. It is the skill of changing a colour very, very gradually so that you can barely see where the colours change. This is called blending. It a skill that will require some practice, so don't be surprised if at first you find it a bit tricky.

Practical activity
※ Show the children the illustration above and point out how the colours gradually go from one shade to the next. Tell them this is what they are aiming for.

※ Ask them first to mix up about a teaspoon of cyan in the palette and paint a stripe across the top of the paper from one side to the other in a pure cyan. Demonstrate.

※ Next, tell them to add the tiniest amount of lemon yellow, transferring the paint on the very tip of the brush, into the cyan.

※ Test the new colour out on the test paper to make sure it is a slightly different colour. If it the colour hasn't changed, tell them to add a tiny bit more lemon yellow and test it out again.

※ Tell the children they must always test the colour on their test papers before they use it, to compare against the previous colour. This will also help to develop their awareness of the subtle differences between colours. If the colour has changed too much, they need to add a bit more cyan back into the mixture. They will need to do this subtle adjusting and comparing of colour throughout the activity.

※ Now they should paint a stripe of the new colour, which should be just a shade different, so that it slightly overlaps the cyan stripe. This will ensure that the colours blend a little at the join. Children will need to be careful not to make their paint too watery and that they paint the new stripe each time before the first one is bone dry, as again this will help the blend. They will need to work quite fast and keep on task in order to achieve the best effects.

※ You may need to demonstrate this technique.

※ Next, the children should add a little more lemon yellow to the same mixture, test the new colour first on the test paper and, if it is just a little different from the last colour made, paint a stripe just slightly overlapping the previous stripe.

※ They should continue down the paper, aiming to not get to pure lemon yellow before the last stripe.

※ Older or more able children could be given a longer piece of paper and challenged to not reach yellow before the end. This colour mixing can be done with any two colours.

Making a collage using work from the previous lesson

USING SKILL

Time
1 hour
Resources
Newspaper to cover tables
Glue sticks
Scissors
Poly envelope for each child
Sketchbooks
Pencils
Envelopes
For the teacher:
A2 paper to demonstrate
Blu-Tack
Access to Richard Lohse picture
entitled: 'Thirty vertical systematic
colour series with red diagonals'
National Curriculum
2a, 4a,b, 5c

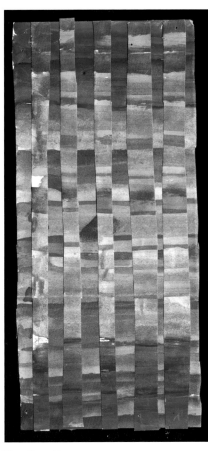
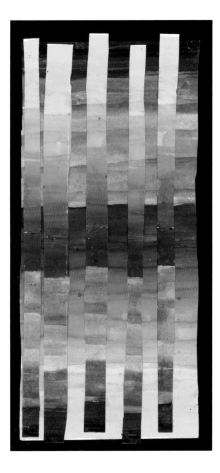

Year 6 pupil

Introduction
We are going to use the colour changes you painted yesterday to make collages.

Practical activity
* Show the children the collages illustrated here and discuss how the colours show up dramatically when they are against a different background, and how different dark colours look against light and light colours look against dark. Show them Richard Lohse's picture if you have it.
* Explain that they are going to make something similar.
* Tell the children to fold their artwork from the previous lesson in half so that the fold goes across the colour stripes.
* Next, the children should cut along the fold so they have two pieces of paper of roughly the same size.

Fold line

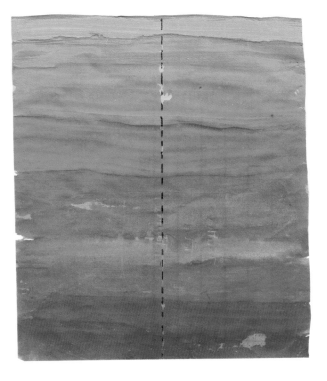

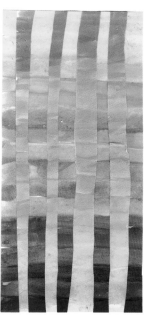

Piece A

Piece B cut into
1cm strips

1cm strips glued
onto piece A

1cm strips glued onto
a piece A of a different
colour background

* Ask them to write their names immediately on the back of each piece. If this is not done, it will very quickly become impossible for children to tell whose strips of colours are whose.
* One piece (call it piece A) should be put away in the envelope.
* Tell children to take the other piece (call it piece B) and cut it into as many strips of about 1cm in width that they can, lengthwise (across the stripes).
* They may need to rule lines on the reverse to help them see where to cut.
* Tell them to write their name on the backs of all but one of the strips and put them in their envelope, and to stick the other strip into their sketch books. They should then label it in their sketchbook, saying which two colours they used, eg brilliant blue and crimson.

* They should now have some 1cm strips of paper with short colour change stripes going across each.
* Lastly tell children to take piece A out of their envelopes and arrange their 1 cm strips from piece B on to it, top-to-tail (darkest to lightest, alternating) with a space between each (see diagram above). Demonstrate this, by Blu-Tacking a set of strips and fixing it up on the board for the class to see.
* The children then glue their arrangements down.
* Lastly, show the children the picture by Richard Lohse (if you can access it) and they could see how it relates to their work.
* If the children have done more than one set of colours, eg reds to blues or blues to yellows, they can use the other colours to make a multi-coloured collage in the style of Richard Lohse.

USING SKILL

Making a collage using work from the previous lesson (simpler version)

Time
1 hour

Resources
Newspaper to cover tables
Glue sticks
Scissors
Envelope for each child
Sketchbooks
Compasses
Pencils

For the teacher:
A sharp craft knife

National Curriculum
2,a 4a,b, 5c

Megan Widlake, Year 6

Note
Children will need two sets of colour changes, from the lesson on page 41. If children are going to use the craft knives, you will need to carry out a risk assessment in line with the school policy.

Introduction
We are going to use the colour changes you painted yesterday to make collages.

Practical activity
※ Show children the collages illustrated here and discuss how the colours show up dramatically when they are contrasted against another range of colours.
※ Tell the children to turn their two papers over and to use their compasses to draw five concentric circles on the back of each.

※ This will give them four rings to cut out, leaving a small circle in the middle.
※ Next they will need to cut out the rings as carefully as they can, causing as little damage as possible to the paintings. Younger children may need to have them cut out for them, but more able children should be able to cut the circles with scissors if a slit has been made for them first with a craft knife.
※ The children can now reassemble new circles by swapping alternate coloured rings with the other coloured rings.
※ If the rings are rotated slightly the colours contrast even more.
※ The pictures could be framed with strips of colours from a third colour series.

Making and using black paint

SKILL

<table>
<tr><td>
Time
20 min (1 hour if doing a painting)

Resources
Newspaper to cover tables

Per pair of children:
Powder paint or ready-mixed colours:
<ul>
<li>crimson + brilliant blue</li>
<li>cyan + lemon yellow</li>
<li>brilliant yellow + vermilion</li>
</ul>
If making grey as well, white paint
1 water pot
1 palette

For each child:
1 medium long-handled brush
Sketchbooks
Test papers
A pencil

National Curriculum
2a, 4a (5a)
</td></tr>
</table>

BB+C→ X BB+CB+C+V
BY+LY

BB+C+V X

BB+C+V

BB+C+V+BY

BB+C+V+BY+LY

BB+C+C+V+BY+
LY

Year 6 pupil

Introduction

It is almost impossible to make your own truly black paint, but you can try to make a 'near black'. There are actually many different types of near black, and if you have ever tried to match trousers, a top, socks and shoes all in the same black you will see what I mean – some will be a slightly bluey-black, some a slightly greeny-black, some a slightly browny-black and so on. It is only a subtle difference, but it is there nevertheless. The blacks in artists' paints actually have different names, such as Lamp black, Ivory black and Mars black, and there are more. You are going to try to mix your own blacks. You will need to record the colours as you go along so you know how you made them and could make them again if you needed to. You will be painting a picture all in very dark colours and in your own blacks.

Practical activity

❋ Suggest that the children start by mixing some brilliant yellow and then add vermilion and ultramarine.

❋ Tell them that the quantities have to be right, and they may need to go on adding first one and then the other for a while.

❋ Explain that if the colour turns blue, then add more red, and if it is too brown, add more blue.

❋ When children have achieved a kind of black using this colour combination, ask them to experiment with other colour combinations.

❋ Remind them to record as they go.

❋ Explain that blacks they have made themselves will go better with other colours in a painting; ready-made black looks artificial.

❋ If they have time, they could try adding white to their own blacks to create a range of different greys. Greys made with ready-made black will all be different shades of the same grey – just lighter or darker, depending on the proportions of white to black – whereas grey made with their own blacks will be different kinds of grey: brown-grey, slate-grey, dove-grey, etc.

❋ Having created a range of blacks, children could go on to paint a picture all in sombre tones. They will usually have lots of ideas for subjects, probably with a spooky theme.

Adding black to make darker colours

Amy Webber, Year 6

Time
30 min for activity 1; 1 hour for
activity 2

Resources
Newspaper to cover tables

Per pair of children:
Powder paint or ready-mixed colours:
- 2 reds: vermilion and crimson
- 2 blues: brilliant blue and cyan
- 2 yellows: brilliant and lemon yellow
- black
1 water pot
1 palette

For each child:
Choice of brush sizes
1 piece of A4 paper or sketchbooks
for recording colours
1 piece of cartridge paper
Test papers

National Curriculum
2a, 4a,b, 5a

Introduction
*Sometimes you need a darker shade of a colour – a darker
green for leaves in the shade, or a darker brown for a tree.
There are two ways to make a colour darker: you can add
other colours to it or you can add black to it. That is the way
we are going to try out today. You are going to try adding
black to colours by gradual degrees to see what new colours
you can make – and then, if there is time, you can paint a
picture using these dark colours.*

Practical activity 1
❋ Explain to the children that first they will
practise making darker tones of a colour.
They will do this adding a very small amount
of black at a time.
❋ Say you suggest they start with vermilion as
it is a mid-tone colour.
❋ Ask the children to mix up some black in their
palettes, then paint a dab of black on a piece
of paper or in sketchbooks.
❋ Next, tell them to add just enough vermilion
to the black to make a slight change from
pure black. Test the colour against the black
to judge the change. Paint a dab of that
colour.
❋ Now add a little more vermilion, check the
tone and paint a dab of it.

❋ Continue adding vermilion and recording the
new colour until pure vermilion is reached.
Now children should have the complete
range of tones, from black to vermilion.
Some children may have ten or more colours,
whereas others may manage only four or five,
depending on age, ability and the degree of
care taken.
❋ Children could add other colours to black in
the same way and record the transition from
black to a pure colour and all the tones in
between.

Practical activity 2
❋ Now ask the children to think of a subject
that might look good painted in dark tones
and give them a time frame to complete their
paintings.
❋ Remind them to use the best brush for
the job, to use their test papers to test the
colours and to aim to leave no white spaces.
❋ Possible subjects could include: spooky
scenes, the woods at night, portraits in
sombre lighting and mood, thunderstorms,
winter evening.

Mixing greys

SKILL

Time
45 min

Resources
Newspaper to cover tables

Per pair of children:
Powder paint or ready-mixed colours:
- black and white
1 water pot
1 palette

For each child:
1 medium long-handled brush
A4 cartridge paper
Test papers

For the teacher:
A2 paper to demonstrate and tape to
fix it to the board

National Curriculum
2a, 4a,b

Catherine Dixon, Year 6

Introduction
Today you are going to mix every shade of grey possible using black and white, from darkest to lightest. You can use the frame of the painting to practise going from black to white, and in the middle area you can paint shapes in different shades of grey.

Practical activity
* Show the children the illustration above and point out how the colours gradually go from black to white and back again around the border. Children may be surprised how many shades of grey there are.
* Tell them to start with black and add a little white at a time until they make a shade of dark grey that is just one shade lighter then black.
* Remind them to test out their greys on test papers before painting with them.
* Explain that it is much, much harder to control the change in colour if they start with white and add black.
* Suggest that they start with black in one corner and then paint one shade lighter grey all along the edge until they get to the opposite corner, by which time they should have reached white.
* Repeat on each side, always starting at black and going to white.
* In the central area, they should make a design of geometric shapes in different sizes.
* Challenge children to never paint the same shade of grey next to each other. The greys could be evenly spread across the painting, or light greys could be on one side and dark greys on another; or it could start dark in the middle and get lighter as it gets nearer the frame. Children will have their own ideas.
* Explain that they have just mixed pure grey using black and white, but there are many other kinds of grey. If they add just a touch of another colour, for example yellow or blue, they will get a different grey.
* Children who have finished their pictures could mix and record other greys, eg browny-, purply- greeny-greys, etc.

Mixing and painting only in greys

USING SKILL

Time
45 min

Resources
Newspaper to cover tables
Some black and white newspaper
photographs

Per pair of children:
Powder paint or ready-mixed colours:
• crimson + vermilion
• cyan + brilliant blue
• brilliant yellow + lemon yellow
• black and white
1 water pot
1 palette

For each child:
1 medium long-handled brush
A4 cartridge paper
Test papers

National Curriculum
2a, 4a,b, 5a

Emily Hewitt, Year 5

Introduction
You have mixed every possible shade of grey, from darkest to lightest, and now you are going to paint a picture all in different greys and black and white. It is possible to paint entirely in shades of grey and for the painting to be as clear and 'readable' as if it were in full colour. If you think of a black and white photograph from a newspaper, you will realize what I mean. You can also mix in tiny amounts of other colours if you want to make different kinds of grey as well as different tones of grey.

Practical activity
❋ Children could copy a photograph from a newspaper of a subject that interests them. This will help them to focus on painting in greys rather than worrying about the composition. Alternatively, they could make a composition of their own, appropriate to the colour. Examples include:
  • A thunderstorm at sea
  • Foggy evening in the city
  • A November morning
  • A factory scene with smoking chimneys
  • A village covered in volcanic ash
❋ Tell the children that they can paint all in blue-greys or brown-grey, or a mixture of different greys, or simply in greys made using black and white. Suggest that they think about what kinds of greys would be most appropriate to their subject.
❋ Remind them to test out their greys on test papers.
❋ Explain again that it is much harder to control the change in colour if they start with white and add black.
❋ Challenge the children to paint some areas of their picture in greys that blend gradually from dark to light – the sky, for instance.
❋ Detail or texture could be added with a fine brush in black or white when the paint is dry.

Creating skin tones

SKILL

Time
30 min

Resources
Newspaper to cover tables
Scissors
Glue sticks

Per pair of children:
Powder paint or ready-mixed colours:
• crimson + vermilion
• cyan + brilliant blue
• brilliant yellow + lemon yellow
• white
1 water pot
1 palette

For each child:
1 medium long-handled brush
A4 cartridge paper or sketchbook
A pencil
Test paper
Coloured pictures of faces from
magazines

For the teacher:
A3 piece of paper to demonstrate the
process, and tape to stick it up

National Curriculum
2a, 4a, 5a

Jeff Hewitt, Year 5

Note
This activity is more appropriate when the children have covered most of the colour mixing lessons, as it will require all their colour mixing skills. Also, some forethought needs to be given in consideration of vocabulary that will be used to describe different skin colours.

Introduction
Today you are going to mix a range of skin colours. You will try to mix your own skin colour, and try to mix the skin colours of people different from yourselves. This will be very useful when you come to paint portraits. You will need to record how you made the colours as you go along, so you could make them again. It is possible to buy ready-mixed paints in skin tones, but you are going to mix your own.

Practical activity
❋ Tell the children that they will need to devise a system and a code for recording
❋ Ask them to cut a square of skin colour from the magazine picture and stick it on their paper with a good space around it.

❋ Go over these pointers in mixing skin tones and explain that they all need slight adjustments to match:
  • A little of crimson or vermilion with a lot of white and a touch of yellow and the teeniest touch of blue will make a pale skin tone.
  • Warm brown and some white make a darker skin tone. Small touches of other colours will vary the shade.
  • Cream can be made with white and brilliant yellow and a touch of red.
  • Crimson and white make good pinks but not good skin tones.
❋ Ask children to experiment to achieve the skin tone, putting dabs of their mixed colours next to the square of their photograph to help them check the closeness of the match.
❋ Remind them how to make a colour lighter without using white (pages 29–30).
❋ They could try to match their hand colour.
❋ If there is time, suggest they try to mix other skin tones.

SKILL Painting a portrait using skin tones

Time
1–2 hours

Resources
Newspaper to cover tables

Per pair of children:
Powder paint or ready-mixed colours:
• crimson + vermilion
• cyan + brilliant blue
• brilliant yellow + lemon yellow
• white
1 water pot
1 palette

For each child:
A choice of brush sizes
A4 cartridge paper or sketchbook
Test paper

For the teacher:
Access to a variety of portraits by
Modigliani
A3 piece of paper to demonstrate the
process, and tape to stick it up
Information about Modigliani (page
102)

National Curriculum
2a, 4a, 5a

Daisy Perham, Year 6

Introduction

Today you are going to use your skills in mixing and matching skin tones to paint a portrait in the style of Modigliani, an Italian painter who was influenced by African masks and sculptures. This is why his portraits often have elongated faces, long necks and almond-shaped eyes that tend to have no iris or pupils. His models tend to look fed up or rather resigned. This could be because many were servants and poor people, but even his friends were painted in a similar style. Children might like to know that the sitters in Cézanne's portraits also rarely smile; this is because he took a long time to paint a portrait and they got fed up.

Practical activity

✳ If possible, the children can look at examples of Modigliani's portraits to discuss his style.
✳ Using an HB pencil or a very pale paint and a fine brush, they should mark out an oval face and long neck that fill the page. Sloping shoulders could be added if there is room. You may need to demonstrate this and help less able children.
✳ Next, the children should lightly draw in an elongated nose which extends in a sweeping

line into eyebrows, and then almond-shaped eyes. Tell them to draw no irises, pupils or eyelashes.
✳ Now they should put in the hairline and the mouth. Challenge them to draw a sad mouth but not a turned-down one.
✳ Ask children to mix some skin colours on their test papers using the notes they made last time, and suggest they try to paint in thin colours, using just a little colour and no white.
✳ Tell them to vary the skin tone so that it is slightly darker on the neck and in the eye sockets, and slightly paler down the nose and forehead, to create the illusion of three dimensions.
✳ Encourage the children to mix a natural mouth colour, using maybe a blend of the two reds and a touch of brilliant yellow, and then paint the mouth in a watered-down version of this colour, again varying the tone to create highlights.
✳ Next, the children should paint the eyes all one colour, with no whites.
✳ Lastly, they should paint the background, having considered the colour and whether it will be all one colour or textured in some way.

Colour matching

SKILL

Time
1 hour

Resources
Newspaper to cover tables
Glue sticks
Scissors

Per pair of children:
Powder paint or ready-mixed colours:
- 2 blues: brilliant blue and cyan
- 2 reds: vermilion and crimson
- 2 yellows: brilliant and lemon yellow
- black and white
1 water pot and 1 palette

For each child:
1 medium long-handled brush
1 fine brush
Cartridge paper
Test papers
A coloured photograph from a
magazine; could be portraits, animals,
landscapes, etc

National Curriculum
2a, 4a,b,c, 5a

Year 6 pupil (showing colour testing down the right side of the painting)

Introduction

Colour matching might be very useful to you in life, whether you become an adult artist or not. You could use colour matching skills not just in art or design and technology lessons, but perhaps when you are co-ordinating the colours of clothes or choosing colours for your bedrooms. Colour matching is finding or making a colour that is as near as possible the same as another one. The best way to do it is to look at the colour very carefully and try to work out what kind of colour it is that you are trying to match. If it is a brown, for example, you could ask yourself questions like: 'Is it a dark brown or a light brown?' 'Is it a yellowy brown or a brown that has a lot of green in it?' 'How did they make this colour and what colours did they use?' You could call this 'unpacking the colour'. You are trying to work out what other colours are in the colour, in order to make it yourself.

Practical activity

❋ Explain to the children that they are going to try to match the colours from photographs, as closely as they can.

❋ Tell them to cut their photograph into four pieces. They could be cut in four strips, horizontally, vertically or diagonally, or they could be irregular pieces, rectangular or triangular quarters. Some mixed colour image needs to be on each piece, so that,

for example, a child is not left with a piece of plain blue sky to match.

❋ Next, the children should choose two pieces of photograph that did not touch in the original image, and put the other two pieces away somewhere where they cannot see them again until the end of the session.

❋ Now ask them to stick down the two pieces of photograph in the same position as they were in the original photo, leaving two spaces.

❋ Explain that the idea is that they should paint in the missing areas. They could change or adapt the image if they want to, but the colours must continue as near as possible to the ones in the photograph, particularly at the point where the paint touches the photograph.

❋ Children might like to sketch in light lines connecting the parts of the images, being careful to make things the same size or 'in proportion'.

❋ Remind them to test their own made colours on their test papers and against the photograph. They should hold the test paper, with the dab of mixed paint colour, right next to the colour in the photograph, to see if it matches.

❋ Just for interest, at the end of the session, children could look at the hidden parts of their photograph, and see how closely they matched the original image.

USING SKILL

Using a range of colours in a painting

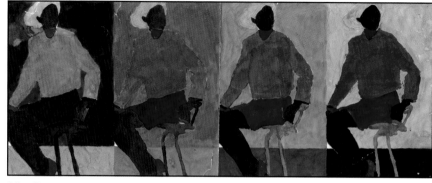
Giles Peacock, Year 6

Time
I hour

Resources
Newspaper to cover tables

Per pair of children:
Powder paint or ready-mixed colours:
• crimson + vermilion
• cyan + brilliant blue
• brilliant yellow + lemon yellow
1 water pot
1 palette

For each child:
1 medium long-handled brush
1 medium- to short-handled fine brush
Cartridge paper
Test paper
An image they can repeat (could be drawn freehand, traced, photocopied or computer-generated)
Access to Andy Warhol's repeated image pictures

National Curriculum
2a, 4a

Introduction
You are going to do a painting and try to use a good range of different colours that you have mixed yourself. Don't use any pure, unmixed colours straight from the pot or bottle. You could look back in your sketchbooks to see how you made different colours and see if you can re-mix them.

Practical activity
❋ Children should look at their repeated image and think about how they will paint each separate image in a different combination of colours.
❋ They could consider changing each colour slightly from one image to the next or more dramatically.
❋ They should divide the background in at least one place.
❋ They could paint the same part of the image in each frame. For example, the hair could be different yellows, the sweatshirt could be different browns, and so on – or they could complete one whole image before going on to the next.
❋ Remind children to test their colours out before they paint with them. If it is not the colour they want, it is generally too late once it is on the painting.
❋ The background colours should be considered carefully as part of the whole colour balance.
❋ Encourage children to think about the effect of one colour against another and as part of the whole.
❋ The children could be shown some of Andy Warhol's repeated image pictures in different colours, such as his pictures of Marilyn Monroe.

Colour theory

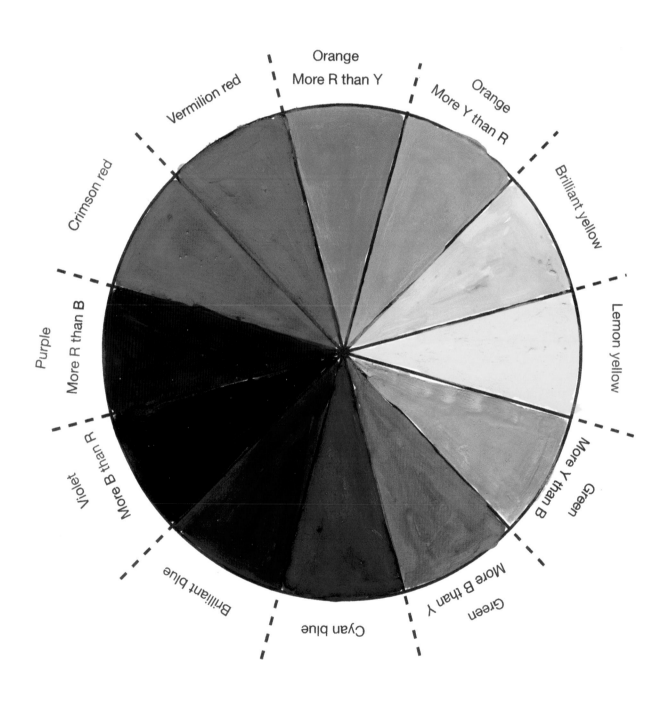

A completed extended colour wheel

Background information

This background information can be read out to the children.

Without light there is no colour. Our main natural source of light is the sun. Colour is not an independent substance on the surface of an object but the reflection of light. Reflected waves of light affect our colour sense.

This is a bit like music and the pitch of sounds; ten vibrations a second means one sound, eleven means another, twelve another, and so on. In the same way, between light made up of waves running at 400 billion to the second and light made up of waves running at 800 billion to the second, there are hundreds of billions of colours.

The spectrum
If we take white light and pass it through a prism, we get a band of colours called the spectrum.

In the solar spectrum (as seen in the rainbow), the colours are not separate and you cannot tell where one colour ends and the next begins. If you simplify the spectrum by dividing it into bands of all the pure colours, you can bend this band into a circle. This is called a colour wheel.

Primary colours
The three primary colours are red, blue and yellow. They are called primary colours because they cannot be made from any other colours. You cannot make a blue by mixing other colours together. You can make different types of blue by adding other colours to a blue, but you cannot make a blue unless you have a blue in the first place. It is the same for red and yellow.

From these three primary colours we can mix all the rest.

Printers use a red that is a deep pink-red and known as magenta, a turquoise-blue known as cyan and a brilliant yellow. When they use these three colours, they can create every conceivable colour.

Secondary colours
Orange, green and purple are called secondary colours because they are made by mixing two primary colours together. Blue and red make purple, red and yellow make orange, and blue and yellow make green.

The colour wheel
Colour wheels are a useful way of showing the effects of mixing paints.

The colours always go round the wheel in the same order, but some colour wheels have more colours than others. In the simplest colour wheel, there are six colours: three primaries and three secondaries. The colours are always arranged so that the primary colours are next to a secondary colour and directly opposite a colour that complements it.

The secondaries are situated between the two primaries that are needed to mix them. For example, orange is always situated between red and yellow. One side of the wheel has colours that look warm (red, orange, yellow) and the other side has colours that look cool (blue, green, purple.)

Simple colour wheels

Warm colours   Cold colours   Warm colours   Cold colours

Tertiary colours
Tertiary colours are colours created using different combinations of all three primary colours. The different proportions make different colours. If red is the dominant colour, a brown will be made, if yellow dominates, then ochre will be created, and if blue dominates it will be an olive colour.

Complementary colours
Each colour on the colour wheel has a complementary colour which sits opposite it on the wheel. When two complementary colours are put next to each other, they contrast with each other and seem more vivid.

Complementary pairs of colours are red and green, blue and orange, and purple and yellow. If these pairs are mixed in paint, they make a kind of grey-brown.

Extended colour wheel

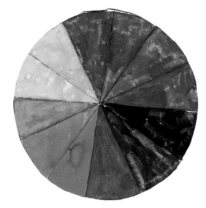

Anthony Scott, Year 6

When colour mixing, if a little of a complementary colour is added to another, it makes a darker tone of that colour. For example, a little purple added to yellow makes a darker yellow. This is useful when painting shadows.

Harmonizing colours
When colours are next or very close to each other on the colour wheel, they are called harmonizing colours because they appear to blend together.

Earth colours
These include browns, greys, blacks, rusty reds and ochre, burnt sienna, raw umber, burnt umber, cinnamon, ginger, etc. Colours in this range are called earth colours.

Hot and cold colours
Pinks, red-dominant purples, reds, yellows, warm browns and oranges are considered warm/hot colours.

Blue-dominant purples, blues, greens, greys and blacks are considered cold colours. Warm colours stand out in a picture and cool colours seem to recede.

Colour moods
Different colours are associated with different feelings, although not everyone feels the same way about colours.

These are some feelings generally associated with colours:
* Red = anger, danger, aggression, heat
* Blue = sadness, depression, loneliness, cold
* Yellow = happiness, cowardice, anxiety, jealousy
* Purple = romantic, poetical, nostalgic, poisonous, royal
* Green = envy, inexperience, youth, spring
* White = innocence, cold, winter
* Black = purity, power, death

There are many more, and often the associations are quite contradictory. This is because colour gets different responses from different people, and also because colours have different symbolism in different cultures.

Artists can use colour to create a response in the viewer by drawing on these associations, which are quite powerful and often deep-seated.

How artists use colour theory to create certain effects
If an artist wants to give the illusion that something is near in their picture, or far away, there are two ways they can do this. One is to use scale, but the other is to use colour.

The further away something is supposed to be from the viewer, the smaller it is shown. But if artists want something to appear to be in the far distance of their picture, they could also use cool pale colours, soft blues or very pale purples – misty colours. If, on the other hand, they want something to seem nearer or to stand out, they could use warm strong colours, such as a bright red or vivid orange.

If they want to draw the eye of the viewer, or to create a powerful or dramatic effect, they might well use two complementary colours together. If they want a peaceful, calm image, they might use lighter tones of harmonious colours.

They can actually break all the rules of colour theory and still create one of these illusions.

Tone in colour
A colour can be made lighter or darker in tone in two ways.

The first way is by adding white gradually. This will make a colour lighter and lighter by degrees. Black can be added in the same way, to make it darker.

The second way is achieved by using less pigment (paint) and more water.

If you have just a touch of a colour on a wet brush and paint with it, it will make a pale version of that colour, as the white of the paper shines through the colour and acts in the same way as the white paint to make the colour lighter in tone.

This takes more skill and control, but the colour achieved is clearer and less chalky. More pigment and less water makes a deeper and more intense tone of the same colour. It is possible to make many different tones of the same colour this way. Either of these methods could be used for every one of the hundreds of billions of colours, so the possibilities are endless.

Key aspects of colour theory

Primary colours

red   blue   yellow

Secondary colours

green   orange   purple

Tertiary colours

Tertiary colours are made by mixing all three primaries and are mostly variations of brown.

Complementary colours

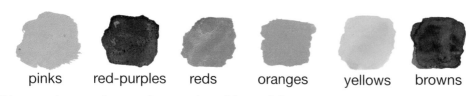

red + green   blue + orange   yellow + purple

Complementary colours contrast.

Harmonious colours

Harmonious colours are close to each other on the colour wheel. They appear to blend when close to each other.

Earth colours

browns   black   greys   rusty-reds   orangey-browns

Warm colours

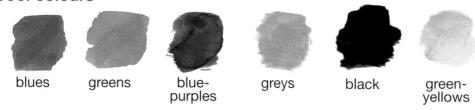

pinks   red-purples   reds   oranges   yellows   browns

Warm colours advance (seem closer) in a picture.

Cool colours

blues   greens   blue-purples   greys   black   green-yellows

Cool colours recede (seem further away) in a picture.

This page may be photocopied for use by the purchasing institution only.

The colour wheel

KEY SKILL

Time
45 min

Resources
Newspaper to cover tables

Per pair of children:
Powder paint or ready-mixed colours:
• cyan + brilliant blue
• crimson + vermilion
• brilliant yellow + lemon yellow
1 water pot
1 palette

For each child:
1 medium long-handled brush
1 short-handled fine brush
Cartridge paper
Test paper
Photocopy of resource sheet 1, page 120

For the teacher:
The colour wheels illustrated can be shown to the children

National Curriculum
2a, 4a

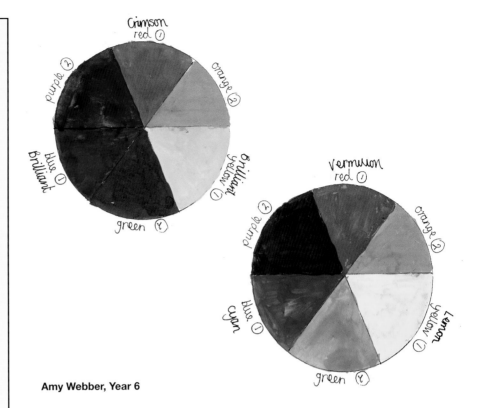

Amy Webber, Year 6

Note
This activity can be done in ready-mixed paint if you have the six colours but it is much better to use powder paint. If children have never used powder paint before, they need to have a quick session in powder paint handling first. See page 26.

Introduction
You are going to make some colour wheels and learn about colour theory and how artists use this to help them to create particular effects. (The information about colour theory on page 54 could be read now, all or in part, to children, but with particular reference to the colour wheel.) The colour wheel is a diagram that helps us to understand more about colours and how they affect each other. You are going to make two colour wheels, the first one using the orangey-red (vermilion), greeny-blue (cyan) and the lemon yellow. You will see the names written on your colour wheels.

Practical activity
※ For younger or less able children put out only the three colours stated.

※ Point out that the colours are written on the wheel and that is where they must paint them in, or the wheel will not be correct
※ The children paint the three primary colours on wheel 1.
※ Next, they mix green, purple and orange and paint these colours in the correct sections.
※ Explain that they are now going to repeat the activity with a different red, blue and yellow to compare the secondary colours created.
※ Repeat the activity with the other colours – crimson, brilliant blue and brilliant yellow – on colour wheel 2.
※ Refer back to the colour theory and ask such questions as: 'What colour is complementary to orange/purple/green?' 'Name three warm colours', 'Name three cold colours', etc.
※ Ask questions such as: 'Which red and blue do you think make the best purple?' 'Which blue and yellow make the brightest or most natural green?'
※ Ask 'What colours would you use if you wanted them to stand out from the other colours or for a poster?' 'Which colours would you use to paint a cold winter's day?'
※ When dry, the colour wheels should be stuck in their sketchbooks for future reference.

The extended colour wheel

KEY SKILL

Time
1 hour

Resources
Newspaper to cover tables

Per pair of children:
Powder paint or ready-mixed colours:
• cyan + brilliant blue
• crimson + vermilion
• brilliant yellow + lemon yellow
1 water pot
1 palette

For each child:
1 medium long-handled brush
1 short-handled fine brush
Test paper
Photocopy of resource sheet 2, page
121

For the teacher:
The colour wheel illustrated with this
lesson can be shown to the children

National Curriculum
2a, 4a

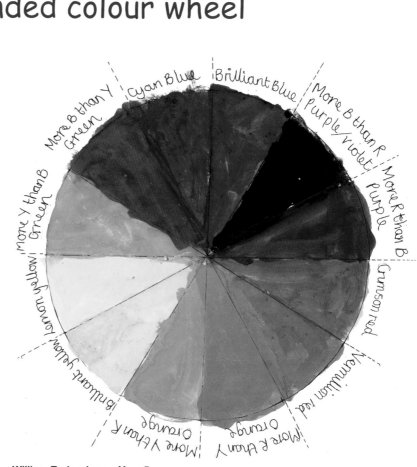

William Taylor-Jones, Year 5

Note
1. This activity can be done in ready-mixed paint if you have the six colours, but it is much better to use powder paint. If children have never used powder paint before, they need to have a quick session in powder paint handling first (see page 26).
2. If children have never made a basic six-colour colour wheel, then they should do one quickly, even if it is just a small one done in felt tips. See previous colour wheel lesson.

Introduction
Today we are going to make a colour wheel and learn about colour theory and how artists use this to help them to create particular effects. The basic colour wheel has six colours, but you are going to make a colour wheel with twelve colours: two reds, two oranges, two yellows and so on.

Practical activity
❋ Children should have access to a basic colour wheel to look at – either one they have made previously, or one up on the board. The one on this page can be shown.
❋ Read out to the children the information about colour theory on page 54, all or in part, but with particular reference to the colour wheel.

❋ Point out that the colours are written on the wheel and that is where they must paint them in, or the wheel will not be correct.
❋ Read the names of the colours around the colour wheel aloud and make sure children understand that when they are mixing the secondary colours, they must make one of the two primary colours dominate. For example, with the two greens: the one nearest the yellow must have more yellow than blue and the one nearest the blue must have more blue than yellow. This will give them both a yellowy-green and a bluey-green.
❋ Encourage the children to use their test paper to try out a little dab of each colour before they paint in the section on the wheel, just in case the shade is not as they want it.
❋ Refer back to the colour theory and ask such questions as: 'What colour is complementary to orange/purple/green?' 'Name three warm colours', 'Name three cold colours', 'What colours would you use if you wanted them to stand out from the other colours or for a poster?' 'Which colours would you use to paint a cold winter's day?'
❋ When dry, the colour wheels should be stuck in their sketchbooks for future reference.

SKILL

Recording tones in colour on a colour wheel

Time
1 hour

Resources
Newspaper to cover tables

Per pair of children:
6 powder paint or ready-mixed colours:
- 2 reds: vermilion and crimson
- 2 blues: brilliant blue and cyan
- 2 yellows: brilliant and lemon yellow
1 water pot
1 palette

For each child:
1 long-handled brush for mixing
1 medium fine short-handled brush
Copy of resource sheet 3, page 122
Test paper

For the teacher:
A2 piece of paper to demonstrate
Masking tape to fix it to the board

National Curriculum
2a, 4a

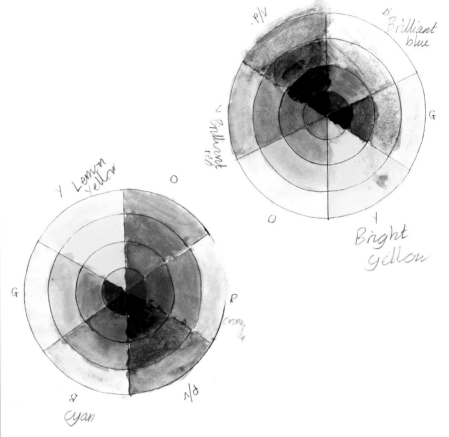

Simon Green, Year 5

Introduction

Every colour has its own full value – that is to say, the colour it will go when it is mixed to its strongest, and painted with the least amount of water. Colours can always be made lighter by adding white, but this can make the colour seem a bit chalky or dull. The way to make a colour a lighter tone without using white is to use more water and less paint (pigment). This allows the white of the paper to shine through the paint, and it is this that gives it its lightness. The colour becomes 'translucent', which literally means the light (or lightness of the paper) travels through it. Today you are going to make four different tones of both the blues, both the reds, both the yellows and the secondary colours they make when mixed.

Practical activity

❋ Ask the children to use the long-handled brush to mix up whichever colour they want to start with. As a general rule it is a good idea to start with a yellow, as the darker colours make the water dirty quicker.

❋ If they are using powder paint, remind the children that the paint needs to be at least the consistency of cream if it is to give its full value.

❋ Next, the children should make a dab of paint on the test paper to check the colour is as strong and deep as it will go. Demonstrate just how strong the colour can be (the full value).

❋ Now tell them to use the fine brush to paint this deepest tone in the centre segment of the colour wheel, where the labelling on the resource sheet indicates.

❋ Next, ask them to experiment on their test papers to see what happens if they use a little less pigment (powder or ready-mixed pure colour) and a little more water. Explain that they can vary the tone by controlling the proportion of pigment to water.

❋ Tell the children that they will need to control the amount of water so that the paint is a light tone but not too runny. This might require some practice and a demonstration.

❋ Once they have experimented, challenge them to create three tones of that colour, going from deeper to lighter, from the inner to the outer three segments of the wheel.

❋ This should now be repeated with all the remaining eleven colours.

Revisiting and extending knowledge of colour theory

USING SKILL

<table>
<tr><td>

Time
1 hour

Link: Science

Resources
Newspaper
Powder paint in 6 colours:
- 2 reds: vermilion and crimson
- 2 blues: brilliant blue and cyan
- 2 yellows: brilliant and lemon yellow

Water pots
Palettes
Medium and fine brushes
Test papers
A3 photocopies of resource sheet 4, page 123
A colour wheel to show, from the lesson on page 57 or colour wheels in their sketchbooks from previous lesson

National Curriculum
4a,c
</td></tr>
</table>

The colour wheel   Hot colours   Cold colours

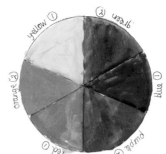   

Complementary colours

Harmonious colours
Take any two colours that are next to each other on the colour wheel and make three of each. For example:

3 greens and 3 blues or	3 blues and 3 purples or
3 purples and 3 reds or	3 reds and 3 oranges or
3 oranges and 3 yellows or	3 yellows and 3 greens or …

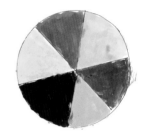

Year 5 pupil

Note
For younger or less able children, or if it is likely that they may not remember which colours are complementary, harmonious, etc, photocopy the key points from the colour theory on page 54 and ask the children to stick this information in their sketchbooks. Alternatively, you could write the key points on the board.

Introduction
Today we are going to look at colour wheels to remind ourselves about colour theories, and we are going to think more about how artists use these theories to help themselves create particular effects in their paintings. We will be painting a colour chart which has a lot more colour information on it. It should be helpful to you when you are creating your own paintings on other occasions.

Practical activity
* Go over the colour theory information which is on page 54.
* Give out resource sheet 4.
* Discuss the various sections of the worksheet and what colours the children will put where.
* Revise names of colours: cyan, vermilion, crimson, etc.
* The children now paint in all the colours on the worksheet. If they forget which colours are primary and secondary, complementary, harmonious, and so on, remind them that

the information is on the board or in their sketchbooks.
* Explain that in each 'complementary colours' section, they should do a different pair of complementary colours, eg one section would be: red green red green red green.
* Remind the children to try out a little dab of each colour on their test papers to check that it is the colour they want. Encourage them to change their water when they need to.
* Suggest that they choose to paint a section that is not next to a painted section that is still wet. Ask them why this is (the colours might run).
* Tell the children to try to keep inside the lines and remind them to make sure they have the right size brush for the job.
* Colour charts should be stuck in sketchbooks for later reference.

Earth colours

SKILL

Time
1 hour

Resources
Newspaper to cover tables

Per pair of children:
Powder paint or ready-mixed colours:
- cyan + brilliant blue
- crimson + vermilion
- brilliant yellow + lemon yellow
- black + white
1 water pot
1 palette

For each child:
1 medium long-handled brush
1 short-handled fine brush
Cartridge paper or a copy of resource
sheet 5, page 124
Test paper

National Curriculum
2a, 4a

Amy Webber, Year 6

Introduction

Earth colours, as the name suggests, are the colours that you would find in the earth. Soil can be many different colours. In some parts of the country, particularly Somerset and Devon, it is a rusty red, while in the Fenlands in East Anglia, soil is almost black, and in some places in Wiltshire it is a pale, chalky oatmeal colour. In Kent, just beneath the surface it is snowy white – the white cliffs of Dover can be seen far out to sea. Browns, rusty reds, spicy oranges, mustardy yellows, greys and blacks are all earth colours. Generally, these colours are considered warm and natural colours. They are the kind of colours that have been used by people since the earliest times, particularly for decoration, as the colours can be found or made from natural ingredients.

Practical activity

✳ Tell the children that they are going to see how many different earth colours they can mix.

✳ Suggest they start off by mixing three primaries and make a range of browns, and then try to make red-browns, green-browns and yellow-browns.

✳ Tell the children to add a little black to some of these colours, and to see what new colours they can make.

✳ They could also try making some greys by adding a little white to their browns. They could also try to make a cream colour.

✳ Colours could be recorded just as dabs of colour, or the children could paint in the sections of a globe as in the illustration here.

✳ Children might find it useful to record next to their dabs of brown, how they made that brown, for future reference, eg vermilion, brilliant yellow and cyan: V + BY + C.

✳ Children should have the opportunity to use their colour mixing skills in a context as soon as possible, perhaps an autumn wood scene, or a still life with a collection of nuts, shells, twigs, feathers, seed pods, etc.

Painting using colour theory

USING SKILL

Time
1 hour

Link:
Literacy
Similes

Resources
Newspaper
Powder paint in 6 colours or ready-mixed paint if preferred:
• 2 reds: vermilion and crimson
• 2 blues: brilliant blue and cyan
• 2 yellows: brilliant and lemon yellow
Water pots
Palettes
Medium and fine brushes
Cartridge paper
Test papers
A colour chart to show (page 56) or their own colour charts from the previous lesson on page 60

National Curriculum
2a,b, 4a,c

Kingsley Lerwill, Year 5

Introduction
Today we are going to test out the colour theory we covered the other day and you can find out if it works.

Practical activity
❋ Ask the children to look at their completed resource sheets from the lesson on page 60.
❋ Read through the sections of colour theory on pages 54–55 relating to complementary, harmonious, hot and cold, earth colours, colour moods and how artists use colour theory.
❋ Discuss these theories with the children and ask for their own ideas about colour moods and colour associations.
❋ Ask them to think of any colour similes or expressions they know, such as: 'as black as soot', 'green with envy', 'to get the blues', etc.
❋ Tell the children they can choose any one of the following options:
   • Paint in all harmonious colours to create a pleasant mood.
   • Try to create a cold or hot scene by painting in cool or hot colours.
   • Try to paint a landscape and make things in the distance look further away.

• Make something stand out in a painting by using complementary colours.
• Choose one of the colours and try to create a colour mood by painting predominantly in that colour.
❋ Discuss other ideas the children may have; they could choose their own subject matter for the paintings.
❋ Encourage them to cover the whole page, leaving no white background.
❋ When the paintings are complete, hold some up and discuss whether the theory works or not in each painting shown.
❋ Children could make a note in their sketchbook about how well they feel the theory worked and how they could use it more effectively another time.

While some children are clearing up, the rest could be doing the colour theory assessment worksheet on page 65.

Trying out different colour combinations

SKILL

Time
1 hour

Resources
Newspaper
Powder paint in 6 colours or ready-mix if preferred:
• 2 reds: vermilion and crimson
• 2 blues: brilliant blue and cyan
• 2 yellows: brilliant and lemon yellow
Water pots
Palettes
Medium and fine brushes
Cartridge paper
Test papers
Sketchbooks or scrap paper
Could have examples of the work of Kandinsky, Paul Klee, Terry Frost (see note below)

National Curriculum
2a,b,c, 4a,c, 5a

Sita Patel, Year 6

Note
Artists whose work you could show as examples include Paul Klee ('Florescence' and others he has painted in a similar vein), Wassily Kandinsky ('Colour studies') and Terry Frost ('October Tambourine').

Introduction
We have talked about colour theory and how artists use it to help them create different effects. Today you are going to try out different combinations of colours and notice how they change when they are placed close to other colours. Whether colours 'go' or not is a matter of personal preference – one person's ideas about colour can be very different from another's. For centuries, artists have played around with colour. Some artists just paint in coloured shapes; their main focus is how colours behave and what effect they have on the viewer.

Practical activity
 Tell the children to try this out on scrap paper or in their sketchbooks:
  • Paint three circles or squares of orange (not closely together)
  • As soon as colour is dry enough, paint blue around one of the orange shapes, yellow around another and red around another.
  • Discuss how the orange looks different when it is surrounded by different colours. Repeat this with other colour combinations.

* If you have them available, show examples of the work of artists such as Kandinsky, Klee and Frost, where they have painted just in coloured shapes.
* Suggest that the children start in the middle of their paper with a coloured shape (squares or rectangles are the easiest) and then consider what colour they will paint next to it and how big that colour shape will be.
* They now continue to add colours, considering at each stage how the overall effect has changed and what colour they might put next.
* The children could try using complementary colours together and then try groups of harmonious colours; they could have areas of the picture painted in cool colours and other areas where they used warm colours.
* This is a slow, considering activity and children do not need to have covered their paper. It is better if they have painted just a few colours, and have thought carefully about them, than if they fill in their paper without really responding to the colours and their impact.
* Children could look at their work at the end of the session and just quietly think about how they feel about their colours and the combinations of colours they have used.
* They could ask themselves questions such as: 'Which colours stand out?' 'Which colours do I like together?' 'Which bit of the painting doesn't seem to "work"?' 'Why do I think this?' These responses are subjective to the child.

Developing an awareness of tone in colour

 SKILL

Time
1 hour

Resources
Newspaper to cover tables

Per pair of children:
6 powder paint or ready-mixed colours:
- 2 reds: vermilion and crimson
- 2 blues: brilliant blue and cyan
- 2 yellows: brilliant and lemon yellow
- black and white
1 water pot
1 palette

For each child:
Choice of brush sizes
Cartridge paper
Test papers

National Curriculum
2a, 4a,b, 5a

Group work, Year 5 (mostly medium tones, with a few light and a few dark tones)

Introduction

All colours have tones; in fact, no two colours have exactly the same tone. The tone of a colour is how light or dark it is. The lightness or darkness of a colour is often a major part of the overall effect of a finished painting. You can create some unusual pictures by considering the tone of your colours as your main focus. You could, for example, paint in mainly dark tones using colours that have a deep tone in the first place, eg purple, violet, brilliant blue (ultramarine), dark brown or deep green. Or you could paint a picture using dark-toned colours that you have made yourself by adding black to your colours. Alternatively you could paint all in light-toned colours such as lemon and brilliant yellow, light greens and yellow-oranges. Again, you could create your own light-toned colours by adding white to the paints. You could also try painting all in colours that are in the mid-tone range, such as red, green, deep orange, cyan and deep pink. This was very popular in the 1960s.

Practical activity

* Explain to the children that they are going to try to paint a picture all in one range of colour tones, ie all dark, or all light, or all mid-tones.
* Explain that the tones in a picture can change its mood; light tones give a soft pastel effect and dark tones make a picture look stronger.
* Tell them they can choose to paint from one of the following options:

- All in colours with light tones (no white added)
- Any colours but all in light tones made by adding white.
- All in colours with dark tones (no black)
- Any colours but all in dark tones made by adding black
- All in colours with mid-tones (no black or white added)

* It might help the children if you write which colours are in which tonal range on the board, for those children who want to try to paint in one tonal group without adding white or black. (The information is in the introduction.)
* Children could choose their own subject matter appropriate to the tones they have chosen to work in, or they could paint in abstract shapes so that the focus is the colour tones rather than the subject matter.
* Tell them that there should be no white background; they should cover the paper with colour.
* Remind the children to test their colours on their test papers in order to check that the colour is in the correct tonal group before they paint with it.
* The paintings could be (black and white) photocopied when they are dry, so that then the children could see clearly whether they had kept to one tonal range. This could be a focus for assessment.

Assessing knowledge of colour and colour theory

Name _____

Name the three primary colours _____

Name the three secondary colours _____

Which colour is complementary to:

blue _____

red _____

yellow _____

Which two colours make orange? _____

Which two colours make green? _____

Which is the best blue and best red for making purple? _____

_____

Which colours mix together to make brown? _____

_____

Name two cold colours _____

Name two warm colours _____

Name two earth colours _____

Which colour is thought to be a sad colour? _____

Which colour is thought to be a happy colour? _____

Which colour belongs in the gap? _____ with envy

Which colour belongs in the gap? _____ for danger

List the colours in the order they come in the spectrum (rainbow) or, if you have coloured pencils or felt tips, draw a rainbow.

_____

_____

This page may be photocopied for use by the purchasing institution only.

Watercolours

Jason Witheridge, Year 6

Introduction to watercolours

Watercolours are made of finely powdered pigments (colours) to which gum has been added to bind them together. The gum dissolves easily in water and helps to fix the colour to the paper. The colours are pure and translucent and can be built up in layers.

A brief history

Many people think that watercolour painting was invented in the 18th century, but in fact it was a fully developed art form long before that. The ancient Egyptians were using watercolours to illustrate their Books of the Dead two thousand years before the birth of Christ. Medieval illustrators were highly skilled in the craft and the earliest of them used 'pure' (meaning 'transparent') watercolour, while later ones added other substances to make the paint more solid and to create a base on which gold leaf was laid.

The British artist JMW Turner (1775–1851) worked a great deal in watercolours and the medium remained popular right through the Victorian era. Edward Hopper (1882–1967) and others continued the tradition in America, while Edward Burra, David Jones and Paul Nash were perhaps the major English exponents. The Swiss artist Paul Klee (1879–1940), a founder member of the Bauhaus, produced his most significant work in the medium.

Character of the medium

The chief characteristics of watercolour paint are its transparency and pureness of colour. The whiteness of the paper shines through and gives the colours light. The paint should be used thinly and the painter must build up the picture, working through from the lightest tones to the

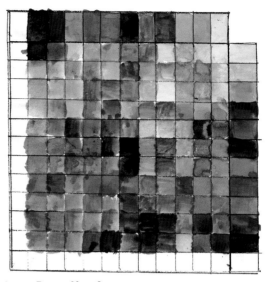

Laura Denzy, Year 6

darkest. Once a colour has been laid, it cannot be easily lightened. Even a very light tone laid over another colour will darken it further by covering more of the white paper underneath. It is this quality of the paper shining through the transparent pigment that gives pictures in watercolours the sparkle and brilliance that sets them apart from other types of painting.

Mistakes can be difficult to correct. Only delicate colours can be washed out with a clean wet brush or a piece of sponge or cotton wool.

In watercolour, only the paper is white; white paint is generally not used. The artist starts with the most delicate colours and adds by over-painting.

Paint

The paints can be purchased in tablets of colour, powdered or in tubes. The tablets, which come in tins of twelve or so colours, are adequate for most needs in primary school. The powder, which is made up with water and generally known as 'Brusho®', is very useful with all ages. The tubes will work out quite expensive as there will be more waste. However, they could be used for art clubs or small groups of children.

The coloured tablets can be bought separately and the spaces in the tins refilled when necessary. The yellow tends to run out first.

Brushes

Watercolours can be best applied with a soft flexible brush.

Year 5 pupils

Buy the best brushes you can afford and keep them especially for watercolours or delicate work. A range of sizes is important, including some big, soft brushes for laying washes. The best watercolour brushes have sable hair and are very expensive, but squirrel hair makes a reasonably priced substitute. There is more information about brushes on pages 12–13.

Paper

Watercolours need to be painted on heavier weight paper than is used for general painting. Proper watercolour paper comes in different thicknesses and with different textures. You can buy it from art shops in blocks, spiral-bound pads or as individual sheets. It will be too expensive for most school art budgets, but heavier cartridge paper will do fine. 190 g/sm (90 lb) or above won't wrinkle too much when painted on. Perhaps a block of watercolour paper could be bought for final paintings at the end of a unit of work, and small pieces could be cut up in advance for children to experiment on.

Proper watercolour papers can be 'rough', which has the most texture, 'not' or 'cold-pressed', which has a semi-rough texture, and 'hot-pressed', which has the smoothest surface.

Dry, damp or wet paper

Generally, watercolours are painted on wetted paper. The paper may just be a little damp or it can be quite wet – it depends on the effect desired. The wetter the paper, the looser and freer the effect will be, and colours will blend and blur into each other. Damp paper allows for a bit more control, and dry paper will leave sharp edges which cannot be removed or dried. It is good for children to experiment with these different effects.

Colours

The following twelve colours, which are generally included in most tins supplied to schools, enable children to mix whatever colours they need: Black, Vandyke brown, Burnt sienna, Carmine (crimson), Vermilion, Prussian blue, Ultramarine, Hooker's green, Leaf green, Yellow ochre, Gamboge (brilliant yellow), White (although it is not often used, it generally comes in the tin).

Useful additions are: Lemon yellow, Raw umber, Payne's grey and Cerulean blue.

I would not recommend the use of masking fluid, as children can have an allergic reaction to it. I had it happen once in a class and I have never used it since.

Daisy Perham, Year 5

Getting to know the colours and the box layout

SKILL

Time
30 min

Resources
Per pair of children:
1 box of watercolour paints
1 water pot

For each child:
1 medium fine watercolour brush
A pencil
Copy of resource sheet 6 (page 125)
or sketchbook

For the teacher:
1 tin of watercolours to show

National Curriculum
2a,c, 4a

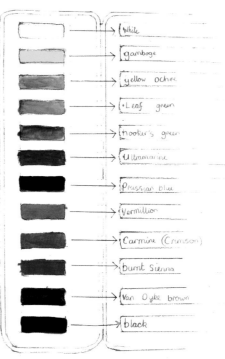

Jordan Wild, Year 5

Introduction
Today we are going to get to know the colours in the watercolour box. The names are a little different from the names of powder and ready-mixed paint. In the tin, some of the colours look very dark, and you might be surprised when you try them to find that they are a dark blue, a dark green or a dark brown.

Before the activity
* Show the tin of watercolours and read out the names of the colours.
* Tell the children that the names of the colours are similar to the names of oil paint colours, and that paint colours are often named after the plant, rock, earth, animal or place they originally come from. However, most paints are made from chemicals now.
* Tell them that the two reds are similar to the reds in powder paint.
* Explain that:
  * Prussian blue is very different from cyan. Prussian blue is a dark greeny-blue which, when mixed with burnt sienna, makes some lovely browns. Prussia is a country that no longer exists (it is now part of Germany).
  * Ultramarine is a blue paint that used to be made from a semi-precious stone called lapis lazuli. It used to be incredibly expensive and only rich patrons could afford to buy it for their painters, but the colour is so good that paintings painted with it 500 years ago are as bright today as they were when they were painted. Ultramarine literally means 'beyond sea' (which is where lapis lazuli was imported from).
  * Raw sienna is an earth colour made from a natural clay containing iron (originally found in Siena, Italy), and burnt sienna is raw sienna that has been roasted in a furnace.
  * Yellow ochre is an earth-colour made from clay containing iron.
  * Gamboge is a gum resin made from various Asian trees. It was once used as a cure for constipation. (They will like that!)
  * Hooker's green is named after the English painter W Hooker, who first used it.
  * Vandyke brown is named after the Dutch artist, Anthony Van Dyck.
* Tell them that they will rarely use the white.

Practical activity
* Ask the children to miss the first space and to paint gamboge in the space below and then write the name of the colour next to it. Tell them to paint the colour as strong as it will go.
* Write the name of each colour in turn on the board for the children to copy.
* Next they should paint yellow ochre, then leaf green and so on, in the same order as they come in the tin. The order may vary according to the manufacturer.
* The completed sheets should be stuck in the children's sketchbooks for future reference.

How to use watercolours and how to make lighter colours without using white

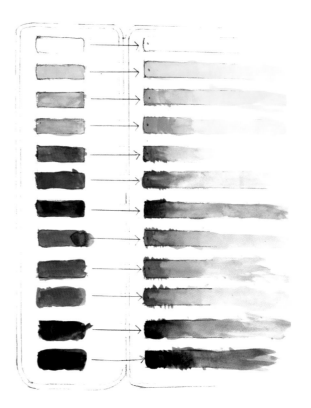

Time
30 min

Resources
Per pair of children:
1 box of watercolour paints
1 water pot
Small palette if required
(not really necessary as the lid will do)

For each child:
1 medium watercolour brush
A paper towel
A4 cartridge paper or sketchbook or
copy of resource sheet 6, page 125

For the teacher:
1 tin of watercolours to show
Paper to demonstrate

National Curriculum
2a,c, 4a

Tabitha Waldon, Year 5

Note
This lesson can be combined with the previous lesson or the one that follows and done in the same session.

Introduction
In watercolour painting, you rarely need to use the white. Lighter colours can be made by using less paint and more water. You don't need white because the white of the paper shines through the paint and gives the colours their lightness. You are going to try to make a full range of tones for each colour from a deep tone, all the way to the very palest tone of that colour. It is a very, very useful skill and one you will be able to use when you are painting.

Practical activity
* Demonstrate how to use the medium:
  1. Wet the brush and blot it on a paper towel to remove excess water.
  2. Move the brush to and fro over the colour until the bristles are covered in paint.
  3. Dab the paint onto the lid of the tin or a palette and repeat until there is enough paint for purposes (for this activity, colours can be used straight from the tin).
  4. Then paint a patch of colour.

* Tell the children not to scrub with the brushes as they will ruin them, and not to leave the brushes standing bristle-end down in the water but always to rinse them and lay them down flat on the table.
* Next, demonstrate how to make the colour go lighter and lighter until you have a pale tone you can barely see.
* Repeat steps 1 and 2 above and then paint a patch of colour.
* Immediately wash the brush, put the wet brush into the patch of colour and pull the colour away from the patch a few centimetres.
* Wash the brush again, put it back on to the place where you left off and pull the colour a few centimetres further away still. Keep repeating this until there is no colour left.
* This is quite a tricky technique, and one that will need a bit of practice. Tell the children that they will have to move fast so that the colour does not dry. Once it is dry, it will have dyed the paper and the colour will not easily be removed.
* Allow them time to experiment and to try it out with a range of colours. The water will need changing often.

USING SKILL

Painting in lighter and darker tones of watercolours

Time
1 hour

Resources
Per pair of children:
1 box of watercolour paints
1 water pot
Small palette if required (not really necessary as the lid will do)

For each child:
1 medium watercolour brush
1 fine brush
A paper towel
A4 cartridge paper or sketchbook

For the teacher:
Paper to demonstrate

National Curriculum
2a,c, 4a

Nicky Loat, Year 5

Note
This lesson can be combined with the lesson on page 70 and done in the same session.

Introduction
In watercolour painting, you rarely need to use the white. You don't need white because the white of the paper shines through the paint and gives the colours their lightness. Lighter colours can be made by using less paint and more water. You are going to try paint a picture entirely in one colour and you will have to think carefully about which parts of your picture need to be dark and which light, before you start.

Practical activity
* Revise how to use the medium.
* Tell the children not to scrub with their brushes as they will ruin them, and not to leave them standing bristle-end down in the water but always to rinse them and lay them down flat on the table.
* Next, demonstrate how to make the colour go lighter and lighter to a pale tone you can barely see (lesson on page 70). Demonstrate if necessary.
* Ask them to choose a subject. This could be topic-led, or a landscape or portrait will give the children ample opportunities to use a wide range of tones.

* Tell children to choose the single colour to paint with.
* The composition could be sketched in using a fine brush ina very pale tone of the chosen colour.
* Tell the children that they must think carefully about which part of their painting will be the darkest and which the lightest.
* Ask the children to consider what the background will be. Will it be dark or light, plain or detailed?
* Explain that they can add more colour to make the tone deeper, but they cannot easily remove colour once it is painted.
* If they are doing a landscape, point out that the sky will probably be the lightest part of the painting.
* When they have been painting for a while, point out that they can add detail and texture with a fine brush over colour already painted and dry.

Painting a 'wash'

Time
30 min

Resources
Per pair of children:
1 box of watercolour paints
1 water pot
Small palette if required (not really
necessary as the lid will do)

For each child:
1 medium watercolour brush
Cotton wool to wet paper
A paper towel
A4 cartridge paper
A pencil

For the teacher:
Paper to demonstrate

National Curriculum
2a,c, 4a

dry paper wash

damp paper wash

Year 5 pupil

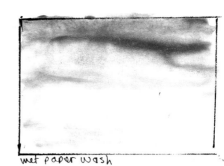
wet paper wash

Introduction

*One of the most important skills in watercolour painting is that
of painting a wash. Watercolour pictures are often built up in
layers, one wash on top of another, and then the picture on
top of that. The washes can form the background, or they can
be the painting itself, depending on the subject. The paper is
heavier than usual painting paper, because it needs to absorb
the water, and it is often wetted or dampened before it is
painted on. You are going to try laying down a wash on wet,
damp and dry paper. The most common use of a wash in a
painting is for the sky, and that is what you will do.*

Practical activity

＊ Revise how to use the medium if necessary
(page 70).

＊ Remind the children not to scrub with the
brushes as they will ruin them, and not to
leave the brushes standing bristle-end down
in the water but always to rinse them and lay
them down flat on the table.

＊ Tell the children to draw rectangles on their
paper as frames for their washes.

＊ Next, demonstrate how to make a wash:
1. Dip the piece of cotton wool in water,
squeeze it out and dampen the rectangle.
2. Mix up some Prussian blue, get plenty of
colour on the brush, then run the side of the
brush across the top quarter of the rectangle.
3. Quickly wash the brush and place the side
of the clean, wet brush at the place where

the colour meets the white paper. Then
run the side of the brush across the paper
and move the colour down the rectangle to
about the halfway point.
4. Wash the brush, place the clean wet brush
on the edge of the blue and pull the colour
down to the three-quarter point; by now
the colour will be a light blue.
5. Repeat the last step and finish off the lower
quarter, covering it with very pale blue
paint. This is the same skill as in the lesson
on page 70.
6. Use a wet brush to spread out and blend
any sudden changes of tone.

＊ Emphasize to the children that they will have
to move fast. If they dawdle, the paint will dry
and they will have a striped sky with bars of
colour instead of a graduated wash.

＊ Next, tell them to try making a wash on wet
paper, then on dry paper. They could compare
the results and experiment. Allow them time to
practise making a wash – it is quite an art.

＊ Suggest that they try to leave some spaces in
the wash to represent clouds.

＊ Tell them to try removing or lightening small
areas of colour with a squeezed-out piece of
damp cotton wool.

Painting a simple landscape with a wash background

USING SKILL

Time
30 min

Resources
Per pair of children:
1 box of watercolour paints
1 water pot
Small palette if required (not really
necessary as the lid will do)

For each child:
1 medium watercolour brush
1 fine brush
Cotton wool to wet paper
A paper towel
A4 heavy cartridge paper
A pencil

For the teacher:
Paper to demonstrate

National Curriculum
2a,c, 4a, 5a

Holly Stone, Year 6

Introduction
*You have practised making a wash and now you are going to
have a go at painting a simple landscape like this one (show
landscape illustration above). You can see that the child who did
this has painted a wash first and then a scene over the top.*

Practical activity
* Revise how to make a wash if necessary
  (page 72).
* Remind the children not to scrub with the
  brushes as they will ruin them, and not to
  leave the brushes standing bristle-end down
  in the water but always to rinse them and lay
  them down flat on the table.
* Ask them to dampen the paper and paint a
  wash using Prussian blue.
* Next, they should mix a little Hooker's green
  into the blue and paint a medium tone of the
  blue-green across the lower part of the picture,
  at an angle, to look like a gently rolling hill.
* Tell them to add a touch of Vandyke brown
  to the same colour mixture to make a green-
  brown and then, using the tip of a fine brush,
  paint one or two trees with little upward flicks
  of their brushes in a medium tone.

* Explain that trees grow upwards and, as they
  do so the branches get thinner and more
  delicate. Say that unless someone has been
  going around with a chainsaw, the trunk of
  the tree will not have a straight, flat top!
* Next, they use a clean wet brush and rub
  it over the branches; the branch colour will
  move a little and create the impression of
  autumn leaves.

Potential pitfall
Children need to be encouraged to use delicate
watered-down colours and not strong colours
straight from the tin. Unless encouraged to do it
differently, they will make tree trunks pure dark
brown and flat at the top, and the upper half
painted in bright green circles; and all the trees
will be standing on top of the hill. They need to be
shown how to be more subtle with their colours
and place trees or other features halfway across
the horizon and foreground and off centre. The
results will be far more 'professional' looking and
they will be very pleased with the results, which
will increase their confidence. Colour mixing
lessons are on the following pages.

Colour mixing in watercolours

SKILL

Time
1 hour

Resources
Per pair of children:
1 box of watercolour paints
1 water pot
Small palette if required (not really
necessary as the lid will do)

For each child:
1 medium watercolour brush
A paper towel
A4 cartridge paper or copy of resource
sheets 6, 7 or 8 (pages 125–127;
whichever is preferred) or squared
paper
A pencil

For the teacher:
Paper to demonstrate

National Curriculum
2a,c, 4a

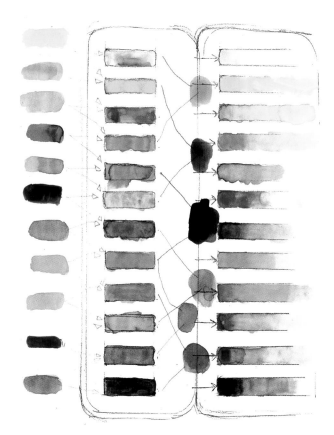

Daisy Waldron, Year 5

Note
If time is short, this lesson can be combined with the
lessons on pages 69 and 70 and so could be done on
the same day and using just one resource sheet.

Introduction
*You have more colours in your watercolour box than you do
with powdered paints, and you are going to experiment with
mixing these colours to make new ones. You can make much
better paintings if you mix your own colours and use a lot of
different subtle colours rather than just paint with colours
straight from the tin.*

Practical activity
❋ Revise how to use the medium if necessary
   (page 70).
❋ Remind the children not to scrub with the
   brushes as they will ruin them, and not to
   leave the brushes standing bristle-end down
   in the water but always to rinse them and lay
   them down flat on the table.
❋ Remind the children to wash their brushes
   between colours and to change the water
   frequently.
❋ Tell them to choose one colour from the tin and
   mix a little on their palettes, wash their brushes,
   choose another colour and then mix the two
   together and paint a dab of the new colour.

❋ The children will need to devise a system of
   recording colours so that they can make them
   again. They could do a version of the art work
   above using resource sheet 6 or try resource
   sheets 7 or 8, or try a coordinates-style grid,
   with the eleven colours along each arm and
   the new colours painted where the coordinates
   meet. An example of this is on page 67. If the
   latter is undertaken, allow more time.
❋ Next they should wash their brushes and
   choose another colour pair.
❋ If children are not using resource sheet 7
   or 8, suggest they try some more unusual
   colour combinations, eg:
   ● Black + Gamboge
   ● Black + Yellow Ochre
   ● Back + Leaf Green
   ● Vandyke Brown + Carmine
   ● Burnt Sienna + Prussian Blue
   ● Carmine + Hooker's Green
   ● Vermilion + Hooker's Green.
❋ Remind them that they can take each of
   these new colours and vary the tone by using
   more or less water.
❋ When dry, the colour mixing result should
   be stuck into their sketchbooks for future
   reference.

USING SKILL

Colour mixing and varying the tone in watercolours

Time
1–2 hours

Resources
Per pair of children:
1 box of watercolour paints
1 water pot
Small palette if required (not really necessary as the lid will do)

For each child:
1 medium watercolour brush
1 fine brush
A paper towel
A6 piece of cartridge paper
A pencil and ruler to mark out squares
1 fine black pen

For the teacher:
Access to Paul Klee's painting 'Cosmic Composition' or 'Red and White Domes' and the drawing 'Home of the Opera Bouffe'
Information about Paul Klee (page 100)

National Curriculum
2a,c, 4a, 5a

Clair Wyatt, Year 6

Introduction
You have tried out mixing lots of new colours and you have learned how to make a colour go lighter and lighter by varying the amount of water on your brush. Now you are going to use both those skills in a colour picture in the style of Paul Klee. Paul Klee was a Swiss artist who, was when he was a young man, was undecided whether to be a musician or an artist. He went to paint in Tunisia while he was trying to decide, and he was so inspired by the wonderful colours there that he made his mind up to become an artist.

Practical activity
✳ Revise how to use the medium if necessary (page 70).
✳ Remind the children not to scrub with the brushes as they will ruin them, and not to leave the brushes standing bristle-end down in the water but always to rinse them and lay them down flat on the table.
✳ Remind the children to wash their brushes between colours and to change the water frequently.

✳ Tell the children to try to fill the paper with squares of different colours that they have mixed themselves, and to vary the tone of the colour within the square.
✳ Children could choose to stick to a family of colours as in 'Cosmic Composition' or a wide variety of colours as in 'Red and White Domes'.
✳ When they have covered the paper and it is dry or nearly dry (watercolour dries quickly), tell them to mix up a dark colour and, using their fine brushes, draw in paint some roofs and doorways, windows, palm trees, patterns and decoration (as in 'Opera Bouffe').

Painting drawings using a restricted palette

USING SKILL

Time
45 min

Resources
Per pair of children:
1 box of watercolour paints
1 water pot
Small palette if required (not really necessary as the lid will do)

For each child:
1 medium watercolour brush
1 fine brush
A test paper
A paper towel to dab the brush on
Children's own drawings of buildings drawn in permanent ink pen

National Curriculum
2a, 4a, 5a

Hettie Pearson, Year 6

Note

It can be a good idea to restrict the children's palette by telling them that they can only use certain colours. It will encourage them to be more experimental with the mixing of their colours, as it will become more necessary for them to mix colours. The artist LS Lowry always worked in just Prussian blue, ochre, vermilion, black and white and he managed to make all his colours using these.

Introduction

You have practised mixing colours and you know how to make a wash, so now you are going to have a go at painting your drawings. Try to use light, delicate colours – just a touch of colour will bring your drawings to life. Too much paint, very bright colours or thick paint will tend to deaden them.

Practical activity

※ Revise, if necessary, care and use of the media and equipment.
※ Remind the children to mix the colours they need and not to be satisfied with the colours in the tin, unless they happen to be the colours they actually want.

※ Ask them to consider the time of day, the season and the weather in their scene before they embark on painting. This will affect the colours they choose. Without guidance, children will often just paint skies bright blue, grass bright green and a yellow sun on the corner of they sky. This is easy for them as they don't have to think about it, but it doesn't make for an interesting or atmospheric painting. Ultimately they will see for themselves that it doesn't look good, but at this age they still need gently nudging away from their comfort zones.
※ Suggest to the children that they leave some spaces in the sky to be clouds. If the sky is to be grey, they should make the grey using a very pale tone of black with perhaps a tinge of yellow, blue or red, but they should not use white and black to make the grey; it will look heavy and dull.
※ Remind them that the sky is usually the lightest part of the picture.

Using colour theory to create the illusion of distance

SKILL

Time
45 min

Resources
Per pair of children:
1 box of watercolour paints
1 water pot
Small palette if required (not really necessary as the lid will do)

For each child:
1 medium watercolour brush
1 fine brush
Cotton wool to wet paper
A paper towel
A5 heavy cartridge paper
A pencil

For the teacher:
Access to colour theory on pages 54–55
Access to some landscapes by Constable, e.g. 'Landscape: Ploughing Scene in Suffolk', 1814
Information about Constable (page 100)

National Curriculum
2a, 4a,b, 5a

David Owens, Year 5

Introduction

You have practised making a wash and learned how to mix a wide variety of colours, and now you are going to have a go at painting a landscape. It will be a simple landscape, just consisting of gently rolling hills, because what you are really focusing on today is using colour in a particular way to help you create the illusion of distance in your painting.

Most painting is an illusion, because it is done on flat surfaces, just the thickness of the paper or canvas, but the image is of something three-dimensional. The artist wants the viewer to see the image as if it really has distance and form. There are different ways an artist can create this illusion: they may use perspective and scale in their picture, they may use tone to give shape and form to a subject, and they can also use colour to help.

In colour theory, there are some ideas that can be used to help create the illusion that some thing is close to you or further away. Bright, strong warm colours look as if they are closer, while cool, pale colours seem to be further away. You
can use this theory to help give your paintings the illusion of distance. If you look at the examples (show Constable landscapes), you will notice that the sky and the distant hills are painted in cool, pale colours, and in the foreground the colours are stronger or warmer. Blue is colder than green, brown is warmer than green, strong green will look closer than pale green and so on.

Practical activity

※ First the children should mark out very lightly with pencil where the folds of the hills will be.

※ Revise how to make a wash if necessary (page 72).

※ Ask them to dampen the paper and paint a wash using a very pale grey with a touch of Prussian blue, all the way down the painting.

※ Spaces for clouds can be blotted out with damp cotton wool.

※ Tell the children start to paint from the back of the picture first, with each hill or field being warmer and stronger in tone than the last.

※ Finishing with some detail painted in the foreground with a fine brush, such as a hedge, trees or fences, will give the painting depth.

※ An empty horizontal band left between the distance and the foreground will give the impression of a lake, as the colour will be that of the wash that was laid first.

Colour mixing with watercolour coloured pencils

SKILL

Time
45 min to 1 hour

Resources
Per group of children:
Box of watercolour pencils

Per pair of children:
1 water pot

For each child:
Sketchbook or A4 cartridge paper
A fine short-handled brush
Pair of compasses and a pencil or
copies of resource sheet 9, page 128

National Curriculum
4a,b

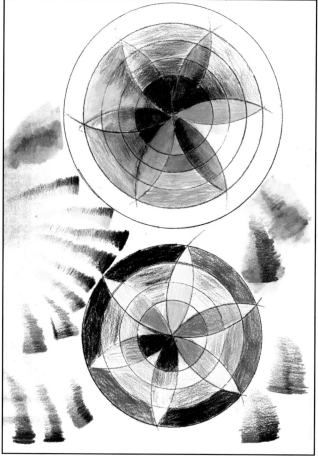

Jack Perham, Year 5

Introduction
You can mix and blend colours with coloured pencils, crayons and pastels as well as with paints. Some coloured pencils and crayons are water-soluble, which means that when they are wetted, the colours move and blend.

These pencils are watercolour pencils, The coloured 'lead' is made up of solid watercolour pigment and, after you have drawn a mark, you can wet it with a brush dipped in water and the pigment will turn into paint, just as it does when you put a wet brush on a tablet of paint in a paint box.

Practical activity
* The children should make their own compass patterns in their sketchbooks if they are not using the photocopied resource.
* First they should try out the different colours in their sketchbooks.
* Show the children how to make a kind of 'tornado' by using the side of the pencil rather than the point, drawing heavily to begin with and gradually getting lighter to get the full range of tones.
* When the children have got the hang of this, tell them to colour in each section of their compass pattern, colouring in the first section the deepest tone and making the next three successively lighter.

* Then tell them to do some tornadoes in different colours, and then draw some more in different colours partly over the top of the first ones. Suggest they try a dark colour over a lighter one, such as brown over yellow, and then a lighter colour over a darker one, to see which blends the best.
* They could try out different colour combinations around the edges of the paper.
* Next, demonstrate how to dip the brush into the water, stroke it on the side of the water pot to remove excess water, and then gently wet the colours with the tip of the brush so that they blend.
* Explain that they will need to wash their brushes between colours, just as they would with paint.
* Tell the children to blend some or all of their coloured tornadoes.
* Ask them to try to make four different tones of a colour within the shapes of the compass pattern.

Acrylics

Year 5 pupils' group work

Introducing acrylic paints

Any paint made from a pigment bound in synthetic resin is commonly known as an acrylic. This term is used whether the resin binder is actually an acrylic or PVA.

Definition that can be read to children
All paints consist of a colour (pigment) and something to bind it together, usually some kind of glue. Acrylic paints are bound together with a kind of plastic. It is quite a recent invention; you could not even buy acrylic paint in Britain until the mid-1960s; it was invented in America.

Acrylic paint is water-based plastic paint that is thick and shiny. It comes in a tube, a tub or a squeezy bottle. You can thin it with water to paint, or you can use it just as it comes. It can even be applied with a palette knife.

Rather like oil paint, acrylic can be painted so thickly that the surface has a texture. Once it is dry, you can paint over the top of it and the new colours won't mix up with the colours underneath. So, you can build up a painting in layers and you can change anything that you want to, but you must wait until it dries. It dries quite quickly, and once it is dry it is waterproof.

WARNING: it will not come out of your clothes, and if it dries on the brushes it will ruin them and they will have to be thrown away. So you must keep acrylic paint off your clothes and wash the brushes out as soon as you have finished with them. You will be pleased to hear, however, that it does come off your skin easily; it washes off when still wet and peels off when it is dry.

A brief history of acrylic paint
The development of acrylic paint came about as the result of pressing social need. In the 1920s, a group of painters in Latin America (mainly Mexico) wanted to paint large murals for public buildings, some of them on exterior walls exposed to the open air. They found that oil paint was unsuitable because it would not last long in such conditions. They experimented with fresco, but this, too, proved impractical.

They needed a paint which would both dry quickly and remain stable in changing climatic conditions. In fact, they needed something which had already existed for some time in the industrial field, but which had not yet been developed as a vehicle for pigments, namely

plastic resins. In the 1930s, scientists and artists worked together to develop new paint formulae, and many interesting murals and paintings were carried out in New York. Experiments continued in North and South America and painters began to realize that the possibilities went far beyond the needs of exterior murals.

In the 1950s, acrylics appeared on the market in America and they played an important part in the techniques of artists such as Jackson Pollock, Mark Rothko and many others.

Research and development continued, but it was not until the mid-1960s that acrylics were available in Britain. Since then, they have been used by innumerable British artists, including David Hockney and Bridget Riley.

Character of the medium
Acrylic paint is water-soluble but, once the paint is dry, it is waterproof. It dries with a shiny surface and can be wiped.

Acrylic paints can be diluted with water to make a translucent glaze, or used as thickly as in oil painting. They can be applied with a brush or palette knife. This makes them an ideal pre-runner to the introduction of oil paints, or as a similar painting experience for children who may not have the opportunity to use oils.

As soon as the paint is dry, it can be over-painted and, unlike ready-mixed or powder paints, the under-paint colour will not mix with the new colour. Paint can be built up in layers and changes can easily be made if children want to alter anything or rectify mistakes.

Potential pitfalls
Acrylic paint does not come off clothes, and if the brushes are not washed out soon after use they will set rock hard and have to be thrown away. Children will therefore need to wear protective clothing.

The lids need to be closed or replaced immediately after use as the paints dry out quickly. Air should be squeezed out of the tubes before replacing the lids.

Possible uses
The colours of acrylic paints do not fade and, as the paints are waterproof, they are ideal for

exterior murals and sculptures. They can also be used for painting areas in a school where they may get marked or worn, such as in corridors. They are also excellent for painting models and other 3-D objects: twigs, stones, stage props, furniture, etc.

Buying paint
Acrylic paint can be purchased at art stores, but most schools' art suppliers stock it, so this will be the cheaper option. It comes in tubes or tubs, and in a good range of colours. Go for the brightest and most vivid colours, plus brown, black and white. Gold, silver, copper and bronze are also available in acrylics.

It is possible to get children to make their own acrylic paints very cheaply by mixing powder paint or ready-mixed paint and PVA.

Special palettes are not necessary (see environmental tip below).

Brushes
Nylon brushes are excellent for use with acrylic paint as they are tough and are easier to clean. Otherwise, the usual long-handled hog-hair type brushes are fine. It is good to have some flat- (chisel-) ended brushes as well as round ends.

Papers and other surfaces
Acrylics are compatible with a wide variety of surfaces; they can be applied to almost any absorbent support, including canvas, wood, hardboard, card or cartridge paper.

Metal
Acrylics can be used on metal but it might be advisable to lightly sand or rough the surface before painting.

Plastic
Plastic acrylics work well on plastic surfaces.

Walls
Crumbling, dirty or powdery surfaces need to be brushed off and made good if necessary, and the area to be painted should be primed with whatever the paint maker recommends (they often have their own recommended primer that goes well with their product).

A useful environmental tip
Lay cling film over the palette, and then put the paint into/onto the palette. At the end of the session, the cling film can be gathered up and thrown away. This will not only reduce the amount of time spent washing up, but reduce the amount of water needed and the amount of chemicals and dyes going down into the drains.

Colour mixing can be done on scrap card which can also be thrown away.

Group work. Designs and painting based on the artwork of the Ndebele people from South Africa

SKILL Using acrylic paints

Time
30 min

Resources
Per pair of children:
1 water pot
1 palette covered in cling film (see note below)

For each child:
2–3 sizes of long-handled brushes
1 thin strip of card
1 plastic knife (for use as palette knife)
A3 cartridge paper
Protective clothing

National Curriculum
2a, 4a

Daniel Huxtable, Year 5

Note: a useful environmental tip
Lay cling film over the palette, and then put the paint into/onto the palette. At the end of the session, the cling film can be gathered up and thrown away. This will not only reduce the amount of time spent washing up, but reduce the amount of water needed and the amount of chemicals and dyes going down into the drains. Colour mixing can be done on scrap card which can also be thrown away.

Introduction
Read the definition of acrylic paint from page 80 or simply explain that acrylic paints are thick water-based plastic paints that can be applied with brushes or a palette knife, and they dry waterproof and slightly shiny. You are going to try out different techniques that you can use with acrylic paint.

Practical activity
* Explain the potential pitfalls to the children (see bottom of page).
* Tell the children to try out the following different effects.
* Use the paint without adding water, and try short brush strokes.
* Paint four patches of thick paint, and in each different patch:
  1. Scratch into it with the corner of a piece of card.
  2. Press the side of the card into it to make a series of lines.
  3. Use the end of the brush to draw spirals and squiggles.
  4. When the paint is dry, over-paint with dabs of other colours.
* Tell the children to mix water with the paint to make it much thinner and to try painting an area in different colours.
* While that is drying, ask them to wash their brushes and use their plastic knives to apply paint thickly, either single colours or several together, so that the paint is raised and textured.
* When the area that was thinly painted is dry, tell the children to over-paint this with patterns with a finer brush, in different colours.
* If there is time, children could experiment with colour mixing.
* Discuss how acrylic paint is different from ready-mixed or powder paint.

Potential pitfalls
Acrylic paint does not come off clothes, and if the brushes are not washed out soon after use they will set rock hard and have to be thrown away. Children will therefore need to wear protective clothing. The lids need to be closed or replaced immediately after use as the paints dry out quickly. Air should be squeezed out of the tubes before replacing the lids.

USING SKILL

Acrylic paints

Time
2 hours

Resources
Per pair of children:
1 water pot
1 palette covered in cling film (see note on previous lesson)

For each child:
2–3 sizes of long-handled brushes
1 plastic knife (for use as palette knife)
A4 heavy cartridge paper

For the teacher:
Access to the work of Maurice de Vlaminck
Information about Van Gogh (page 102)

National Curriculum
2a, 4a, 5a

Daisy Barker, Year 5

Introduction
You have tried out different techniques with acrylic paints and now you can try using some of these in a painting.

Practical activity
❋ Remind children of the potential pitfalls (see bottom of the page).
❋ Suggest some subjects for the paintings. These could be topic-related or inspired by the work of artists whose paintings clearly show strong brush or palette knife marks and who use strong colours, such as Maurice de Vlaminck. A landscape is an easy subject choice. Show some samples if you have them.
❋ Tell the children that somewhere in their paintings they should try to:
  • Use the plastic knife to apply paint, and to over-paint in other colours.
  • Show their brush marks to create a bold, dramatic effect.
  • Scrape marks into the paint.
  • Perhaps use highly thinned paint to over-paint with, to make a coloured glaze.
❋ Tell the children to cover the paper, leaving no white spaces.
❋ Discuss how acrylic paint is different from ready-mixed or powder paint.

Potential pitfalls
Acrylic paint does not come off clothes, and if the brushes are not washed out soon after use they will set rock hard and have to be thrown away. Children will therefore need to wear protective clothing. The lids need to be closed or replaced immediately after use as the paints dry out quickly. Air should be squeezed out of the tubes before replacing the lids.

Painting exterior walls with acrylic paints: a long-term large-scale project

USING SKILL

Time
Stage 1: 30–40 min
Stage 2: 15 min per child
Stage 3: 30 min per child

Resources
Exterior surface to be painted

Per pair of children:
Photocopy of Ndebele patterns

For each child:
Sketchbook or paper
B pencil
Coloured felt tips

For each child:
4B pencil

For a group of 3 or 4 children:
20 or more long-handled brushes, in 2–3 sizes
Acrylic paint in white, black and chosen colours
20 or more paper plates as palettes (3–4 of each paint colour)
Protective clothing

For the teacher:
Internet or other access to images and information about the art of the Ndebele
Another adult to supervise during the exterior work

National Curriculum
1c, 2a, 4a,c, 5a,b

This PE shed was painted 4 years ago, and the paint still looks quite good despite battering by wind, rain and footballs

Note
Before starting the artwork with the children, measure the exterior surface to be painted and allocate an area for each child involved so that they have a shape and dimension to design for. Clean and prime the surface in whatever way is appropriate. A border could be left to frame the work. Prime the surface if necessary (see note about painting on walls and surfaces on page 81).

Introduction
You are going to look at the work of the Ndebele people of South Africa and the way they decorate their houses and possessions, and then you are going to paint (whatever the project is – in the example illustrated, a PE shed in the playground was painted). You will be using acrylic paints, which are waterproof once they are dry and the colours do not fade.

Practical activity
Stage 1: the design process
❋ Show the children the work of the Ndebele people and explain how and why they do this.
❋ Point out some of the characteristics of the designs: the shapes, the colours, the symmetry, etc.
❋ Ask the children to copy some of the patterns into their sketchbooks and then create their own patterns using similar characteristics.
❋ Tell each child the shape of the area their design will be in, and ask them to choose one of their own Ndebele patterns and then adapt it to fit into the shape. They should also plan the colours. Give them a specific selection of colours to work with, but they must include black and white.

Stage 2: drawing on the exterior surface
❋ A group of three or four children could work on different areas at the same time.
❋ Tell the children to copy their own design onto the surface using a pencil, and to write their name or initials somewhere in their area.

Stage 3: painting the exterior surface
❋ Remind the children of the pitfalls (see note at end of the previous lesson).
❋ Start with the white, and tell the children to find their own area and paint in the planned white parts. They should try to keep well within the lines drawn.
❋ Next they should paint the coloured areas.
❋ Lastly, the children should use a finer long-handled brush and paint the outlines of all the shapes in black. They should also edge all the white shapes and borders in black.

Oils

Karen Facey, Year 5. Oil on canvas

An introduction to oil paints

Oil paint is made of dry powder (pigment) colour, mixed to an appropriate thickness with one or another of a number of vegetable oils, usually either linseed or poppy oil. Despite its reputation as 'high art', oil painting is a relatively simple method. Brushes and hands will need to be cleaned in turpentine, and if the paint needs thinning, it can be done with turpentine and/or linseed oil.

A brief history of oil painting

The earliest surviving oil paintings are from 13th-century Norway, but it was the Italian artist Titian (1490–1576) who played a dominant role in developing the techniques and possibilities of oil painting. The Flemish artist Rubens (1577–1640) is also historically important. He had enormous success and influence as a master of successful pupils and assistants, and he laid down a method of procedure with oil paint which, with some variations, was to be followed by generations of painters. This has been the technique most used since the 17th century.

At one time, all artists (or their assistants) would have to make the paint themselves, grinding the pigments and adding the oil. Then, in England in 1789, Thomas and Richard Rowney started a business which was to grow into the modern company George Rowney & Co. In 1832, William Winsor and Henry Newton started the partnership which is now famous, and ready-made oil paints could be bought.

Information that can be read to pupils

All paints consist of a colour (pigment) and something to bind it together, and they all use something to thin it with. In the case of watercolours, acrylics, powder paint and ready-mixed paint, this 'something' is water. However, in the case of oil paints, the 'thinner' as it is called, is linseed oil or turpentine (which is often known as 'turps'). These two are sometimes mixed.

Oil paint is probably the most famous kind of paint that artists use. It takes quite a long time to dry – often several days – but the colours change very little when they dry. The most common surface to paint on is canvas, but you can also paint on wood or hardboard and special oil paper.

The canvases need to be 'primed' before they are used, which means they must be painted with at least one coat of a special primer. You can buy canvases ready primed.

The brushes will need to be cleaned with turps and wiped afterwards with a rag. When all the paint has been cleaned out of the brushes, they can be washed in warm water with some washing-up liquid. The bristles need to be rubbed between your fingers until they are soft. If the brushes are not cleaned properly, they will be no good to use another time.

You can only get the paint off your hands with turps. Water will not get it off, and you will need to wash your hands afterwards to get rid of the strong turps smell. You must also wear something to protect your clothes. Oil paint might come out of clothes with a lot of rubbing with a turpsy cloth, but it may very well leave a mark.

Oil painting is not difficult; if you can manage acrylic paint, you can manage oil paint.

Joshua Derbyshire, Year 5

Character of the medium

Oil paint is oil/turps soluble, but once it is dry it is fixed and hard and will not fade or change. It can be applied thinly if it is diluted with linseed oil or turps, and it can be applied thickly using brushes or palette knives. It takes a long time to dry and children may find this frustrating if they want to over-paint for any reason. However, it is possible to lay a thick layer of paint over another, and the colours will not mix if they are left alone.

Too much movement with the brush will cause the under-layer to mix with the new layer. The thinner the paint, the quicker it will dry.

Children can under-draw and paint over, or paint a drawing with a fine brush to indicate where they want things to go, or they can launch into the painting without drawing first. As they may not have had many, if any, previous opportunities to use oil paints in the primary school, it is nice for them to just 'have a go' and launch into a painting without too much forethought and too much idea of the outcome. This way, the paintings will be more lively and spontaneous. Let them enjoy the medium and explore it as they go along, discovering for themselves what it will and will not do.

An oil painting should be a painting and not a painted drawing. Encourage children to be bold, to use a palette knife and to lay the paint on thickly if they want. Make the experience as different as possible from powder or watercolours.

Buying supplies

Paint and other oil painting equipment can be bought through schools' art suppliers, who will also stock turps and linseed oil. 'Student' grade paint is adequate for primary school use and is cheaper than 'artist's' grade. The paints will often come in a box of mixed colours, but the colours can also be purchased individually.

Palettes

Oil paper palettes will save a lot of clearing up, or pieces of card can be used. If wooden palettes are used, they will need to be scraped clean after use and wiped with a rag dampened with turps.

Canvases and other surfaces

Canvases come in different sizes can be bought quite cheaply from budget shops. Remaindered book shop chains also often stock cheap canvasses. Specialist art shops will probably prove expensive. An A5 canvas is a good size for a first attempt.

Alternatively, children could paint on oil paper or hardboard, or on wood.

Brushes and palette knives

Hog bristle brushes are fine to use, and it is good for the children to have access to flat-ended brushes as well as round-ended ones.

Palette knives are a luxurious extra. If the art budget will run to it, get half a dozen; if not, then use plastic knives.

Colours

These are the basic colours and children can mix a good number of other colours from them:

Titanium white	Alizarin crimson
Cadmium red	Ultramarine
Cadmium yellow	Prussian blue

These could be supplemented by:

Cadmium orange	Chromous oxide green
Cerulean blue	Raw sienna
Ivory black	Burnt umber

Pitfall

Turps has quite a strong smell and some children may find the fumes unpleasant or it could even make them feel dizzy.

It might be a good idea to open a few windows and have some passage of air in the room. Latex gloves should be used for cleaning brushes etc, or it might be better to draft in an adult helper to help with clearing up.

I always imagine my actions as if they were reported in The Daily Blab:

CARELESS TEACHER ASPHYXIATES WHOLE CLASS OF DEAR LITTLE PRIMARY SCHOOL CHILDREN

Oil paint palette

SKILL Using oil paints

Time
1 hour

Resources
Newspaper for the tables

Per pair of children:
1 pot with some turps/linseed oil
1 flat palette (piece of card/wood/
plastic or oil paper palette with a little
of each of the colours of oil paint
squeezed round the outside edge)
1 piece of rag

For each child:
2–3 sizes of long-handled round-
ended and flat-ended brushes
1 plastic knife (for use as palette knife)
Canvas paper or off-cut of plywood
Protective clothing

For the teacher:
Information on oil painting from the
previous pages

National Curriculum
2a, 3a, 4a,b

Oil paint palette

Introduction
*Read the information on oil painting for children on page 86
and then tell them that first they are going to try out using oil
paints before they do a painting.*

Practical activity
❋ Explain to the children that the brushes will
need to be cleaned in the turps and wiped on
the rag between colours.
❋ Say that the paint can be thinned with either
linseed oil (if you have it) or turps.
❋ Tell them that they will be mixing the paint
and colours on the palette and they should
not use up all the space on it in one go.
❋ Suggest that as the materials are expensive,
they should just use small amounts.
❋ Tell them that they should take the paint on
their brush and just make some small brush
strokes on their canvas paper (or whatever
surface is being used), clean their brush and
then try some brush strokes of a contrasting
colour.

❋ The children could paint in small thick dabs,
then thin the paint by keeping a little more
turps on their brush, and then paint a few
strokes in thinner paint.
❋ They could now try mixing two colours by
taking a little of each colour, transferring
these to the middle of the palette and mixing
them there. Remind them to clean their
brushes between colours.
❋ The children can now continue to mix
colours, try them out and try to discover what
the paints will and won't do.
❋ They should try: applying the paint with a
palette knife; over-painting; creating swirls
and dots; long and short brush strokes;
painting smooth flat areas; and using
different-sized and -shaped brushes.
❋ At the end of the session, discuss what
impression the children have of the medium
and what they think will be the pros and cons
of working in it.

Pitfall
Read pitfalls on the use of turps on page 87.

Painting in oils

USING SKILL

Time
2 hours or more

Resources
Per pair of children:
1 pot with a little turps/linseed oil
1 flat palette (piece of card/wood/
plastic or oil paper palette)
1 piece of rag

For each child:
1 piece of charcoal
2–3 sizes of long-handled brushes
flat- and round-ended
1 plastic knife (for use as palette knife)
1 canvas, canvas board or canvas
paper
Protective clothing
Idea or plan for subject or picture to
copy

For the teacher:
If required, some suitable simple
picture for children to copy
Images of oil paintings to show, eg
Van Gogh, Monet, Vlaminck, Renoir

National Curriculum
2a, 4a, 5a

Daisy Barker, Year 5

Note
Before starting this lesson, children need to have decided in advance what they will paint. In the example shown, children painted seascapes, as they were studying water in other subjects. They could try to copy a painting by an artist, or they might have already planned a picture. As this may be their only opportunity to use oil paints, they should not spend too much time worrying about what to paint, but just get on and experience the medium itself. The subject of the painting does not need to be content-led; it could just be colours, shapes and textures. However, the children may well want to paint 'something', so it is as well to have sorted this out in advance.

Introduction
You have tried out handling oil paints and you now know some of the advantages and disadvantages of using them, so now is your chance to paint a picture in oils on a canvas. This painting, when it is finished, should last for a very long time. You or your parents might well still have it in fifty years' time or longer.

Practical activity
* Explain to the children that the brushes will need to be cleaned in the turps and wiped on the rag between colours.
* Say that the paint can be thinned with either linseed oil (if you have it) or turps.
* Tell them that they will be mixing the paint and colours on the palette and they should not use up all the space on it in one go.
* Children should now mark out their basic composition in charcoal (no detail).
* Next, they should flick it lightly with their clean rag to remove surplus charcoal. At this stage, the composition can easily be changed or adjusted.
* When children are happy with their composition, they could start to paint over the charcoal with a fine brush dipped in a thin mixture of a light colour of paint. This will fix the drawing.
* Now they can start to paint in areas. Tell them to work from 'lean to fat', that is to start off blocking in areas in thinner paint and then build up the picture in later stages with undiluted paint and ending with thick, textured paint and palette knife work. They should start with the darker colours and add lighter areas as they go along.
* From time to time, they should stand back from their pictures to view them and make decisions as to how to progress.

Pitfall
Read pitfalls on the use of turps on page 87.

History of painting

Will Ayres, Year 5 (illuminated letter A)

A few key pointers in the history of painting

Note: this is suitable for reading to the children.

Cave paintings (at least 20,000 years ago)

The earliest paintings have been found in caves all over the world. Prehistoric people lived at the entrances to these caves and the paintings have been found deep inside them. There are many pictures of the animals the people hunted, such as bison, horses, stags and even woolly rhinoceroses. From these paintings we know about extinct animals, such as the mammoth. There are various theories about why they were painted, but some historians think they were part of the hunting ritual and would bring good luck in a hunt. Other experts think that the caves where the paintings are found might have been places of worship.

Some famous caves in France were discovered by accident. Some boys were out for a walk with their dog, and the dog disappeared down a hole in the hillside. One of the boys went to search for him. The ground beneath the boy's feet gave way and he tumbled into a cave, followed by his friends. They lit matches to see where they were, and were amazed to find hundreds of animals painted on the walls.

The prehistoric artists used soil and rocks to make red-brown, black, yellow ochre and white colours. They mixed them with clay, crushed them and added water or animal fats to make them liquid. The paints were kept in hollowed-out bones, which were plugged at one end. The artists painted with their fingers or used brushes made of twigs with chewed ends. Pads of fur and moss were also used, and they worked by the light of animal fat lamps.

Egyptian painting (approximately 3,000 years ago)

Survival was the chief preoccupation for prehistoric people, but the people of ancient Egypt had the wealth and leisure to create objects which were ornamental and not just functional. However, survival still played its part, as the Egyptians believed in life after death. Pictures were painted on the walls of the tombs of their kings, and many beautiful objects were placed in the tombs to help the buried kings and queens in their next lives.

The Egyptian artists followed strict rules about the way figures were represented: the head was in profile, the shoulders and eyes were viewed from the front and the legs and feet were again viewed from the side, with their feet invariably being depicted facing the same way. Egyptians believed that this showed the human figure to its best advantage.

The Egyptian artists were specially trained to paint spells on coffins and scenes on the walls of tombs of kings and other important people. People believed the spells would protect the dead, and that the scenes would work by magic to give them everything they needed for living in the next world.

Egyptian artists ground their own colour from minerals and used charcoal (burnt wood) for black and ochre for red. They invented six colours to paint with; before that artists had only been able to use black, white and earth colours (see timeline of colours on page 93).

European illuminated manuscripts (approximately 1,200 years ago)

The pages of medieval manuscripts were often brilliantly decorated with gold leaf and bright colours. These were done by hand by monks in monasteries. The illustrated books took years to produce. Bibles and prayer books were illustrated with tiny scenes, sometimes painted below the writing and sometimes inside the capital letter of the first line of a new paragraph or chapter. The text was often surrounded by beautifully painted and richly patterned borders.

The paints they used were made by the monks or their assistants. They used egg tempera, which is a paint made by mixing egg yolk with the ground powdered colours (pigments). Some of the pigments were crushed semi-precious stones such as lapis lazuli, which is a beautiful blue. Where lapis lazuli has been used, the blue is as bright today as it was when it was painted hundreds of years ago. The blue is a bit like the brilliant blue or ultramarine that we use today and it was as valuable as gold. They also used gold itself, which had been made as thin as tissue paper (this is called 'gold leaf'), to decorate their books.

European art (until about 200 years ago)

The subject matter of most paintings in Europe until about 200 hundred years ago was either religious or portraits of wealthy and important people. Kings, queens, popes, other rulers and churches or cathedrals might commission paintings of religious scenes or portraits of themselves, their families and their property. There were also specific subjects for paintings, such as still life and landscapes, and there were rules about what should be included in the painting and where. The person who asked for and paid for the painting would say what they wanted to be in it – it wasn't up to the artist. Some kings and queens loved art more than others and would have several artists working for them creating beautiful things.

Artists often worked in studios with other artists, and their apprentices mixed paints and learned to paint specific things like folds in clothing, hands or backgrounds.

Artists needed to find someone rich or important who would sponsor them and commission them to do paintings, or a studio who would take them on. They might have to pay for the privilege or find someone who would pay for their apprenticeship for them.

Colours

It is interesting to remember that in the past, an artist's palette was restricted by availability; the colours that we paint with today were not always available, and some were very expensive. Many paints have unusual names. They are often named after the plant, rock, earth, animal or place they come from.

Children might like to hear about these:

* Dragon's blood was the name of a pigment made from a fruit – not, as people thought, made from real dragon's blood.
* Indian yellow was a yellow pigment from India that was made by heating the urine of cows fed on mango leaves.
* Lampblack comes from soot which is made by burning oil or fat.
* Raw sienna is an earth colour made from a natural clay containing iron; burnt sienna is raw sienna that has been roasted.
* Tyrian purple was made from crushed shellfish. This was such an expensive pigment it was used to dye the robes of the emperors in ancient Rome, and purple is still considered to be a royal colour today.

Thomas Corras, Year 5 (illuminated letter C)

A timeline of colours

Some colours are very old and some relatively modern.

20,000 BC	Burnt wood (black) Chalk (white) Ochre (yellow-brown made from earth) Umber (brown made from earth) Other earth colours, eg red-brown
1000–2000 BC	Blue frit (known also as Egyptian Blue) Malachite (green made from copper) Realgar orange (contains arsenic) Cinnabar red (contains mercury) White lead (white) Lemon yellow
100 BC	Indigo (dark blue made from a plant) Tyrian purple (made from a whelk) Verdigris (green)
12–1300 AD	Lead-tin yellow Madder (ruby red made from a plant) Vermilion (light red made from the mineral cinnabar) Ultramarine (blue made from lapis lazuli)
1700	Prussian blue (dark blue)
1750	Naples yellow (made with lead)
1800	Cobalt blue
1817	Cadmium yellow
1820	Chrome yellow
1828	Ultramarine (blue) – a synthetic version
1830s	Zinc white
1856	Perkins mauve
1861	Cobalt yellow
1910	Cadmium red
1916	Titanium white
1918	Cadmium orange

After this, many more colours were manufactured using chemicals, and there is now a huge range of colours available to artists.

Holly Peacock, Year 6

Cave paintings, part 1: making your own paint and charcoal

SKILL

Time: 1 hour

Links: History/Design and Technology

Resources
Newspapers to cover tables
Earth, sieved to remove stones and wildlife (you could use garden-centre soil)
Collection of dry twigs to burn
Lighter/matches
Ice cream tubs to collect and mix earth
Large lump of white chalk (or sticks of chalk)
1 flat stone and 1 heavy stone for grinding chalk
Vegetable oil
Water
Green twigs, feathers, moss, string, grasses, etc

Per group of 4–5 children: 2 water pots to hold paints

For each child: Protective clothing

For the teacher: Access to images of cave paintings/
Nerves of steel/Second adult to assist

National Curriculum: 2a,c, 3a, 4a,c, 5a,d

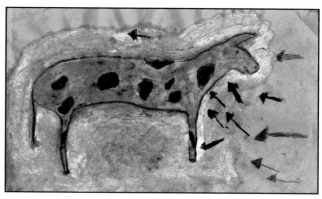

Izzy Merlin, Year 5

Note
Be aware of health and safety issues when making the twig bonfire and when children are handling earth; make a risk assessment and follow school guidelines.

Introduction
Read the information on cave paintings to children on page 91 and show images of cave paintings.

Practical activity
❋ Tell the children that they are going to try making their own paints and their own brushes, just as the cave people did, and that later they will be painting with them.
❋ If possible, go out into the school garden or grounds with the children and collect earth and dead dry twigs.
❋ Also collect green twigs, moss, grasses, feathers and anything else that could conceivably be used or might have been used by cave people to make brushes.

Making charcoal
❋ One adult, and possibly a small group of children, should remain and build a small bonfire of the twigs. This should be left to burn itself out. If the twigs are thin, they will burn up quite quickly.

❋ The cooled burnt twigs can be collected later when the paint and brushes have been made.

Making brushes
❋ Explain to the children that they could make brushes by tying leaves, grasses, moss or thin twigs to a twig handle (they could cheat here and use string to tie the bits and bobs on).
❋ Another way to make brushes is to take a green twig and bash the ends of the twig between two stones until it frays out. Fibres can then be separated further with their fingers.

Making paint
❋ White paint:
  • The chalk should be ground to a powder by crushing it between two stones. Children could also try breaking the chalk sticks into small pieces and crushing them inside a paper towel.
  • Next, the powder should be collected into one pot, and a little vegetable oil and some water added to make a thin paste.
❋ Brown paint:
  • The earth should gradually be mixed with water and vegetable oil until it reaches a paint-like consistency. Powdered chalk or charcoal could be added to make the brown lighter or darker.
  • The paints and charcoal can now be distributed among the children.

Potential pitfalls
❋ Some of the home-made brushes will undoubtedly fall apart during the painting session or will not work as well as they might, especially if children have used too large a twig or have not tightly secured the hairy part of the brush to the handle. These children will need to continue with school brushes.
❋ The children may get carried away when they are mixing up the earth paint!

Cave paintings, part 2 (can be done with or without making your own paints, brushes and charcoal)

SKILL

Time
1 hour

Links
History

Resources
Newspaper to cover tables

Per group of 4–5 children:
Home-made paints, etc
2 water pots to hold paints
A pile of burnt twigs
Home-made brushes
4–5 spare school brushes, in case

Resources if not making paints, etc:
Newspapers for tables
Sticks of white chalk
Charcoal
Brown chalky pastels or
Brown paint, paintbrush and water in pots

For all children:
Protective clothing
Sketchbook and pencil
A3 brown or stone-coloured paper

For the teacher:
Access to images of cave paintings and horses, deer, bison, and wild boar

National Curriculum
2a,c, 3a, 4a,c, 5a,d

George Green, Year 6

Note
This lesson works very well if the children make their own paints, but it also can be done using school charcoal, brushes, chalk, brown pastels or paint. It does have more impact when the children make their own materials, but this can be very messy and time-consuming. Ironically, the end results often look better when they have used shop-bought products. The home-made variety can look like a pig's breakfast, but the children love doing it.

Introduction
Read the information on cave paintings to children on page 91. They could also hear some of the information about the history of colours and the colour timeline on page 93. Tell children that they are going to make some paintings similar to those found in the caves.

Practical activity
✳ Look at the images of cave paintings and discuss the colours and the content. Encourage the children to speculate about how and why the paintings were made and what living conditions might have been like. Discuss the importance of hunting to the survival of the cave people.
✳ Children should now look at images of cows, deer, bison, etc and sketch some in their sketchbooks. (The children that did the work illustrated here went to draw cows that were grazing in a field across from the playground, but the wretched animals went and lay down, so you can't win!)
✳ Next, the children should draw on their brown paper, using their charcoal, one large (appropriate, eg not a guinea pig!) animal of their choice in the middle of the page, and possibly some arrows and hunters.
✳ Tell the children to colour the background white, using either their home-made paint and brushes or a piece of chalk. This will make the animal stand out as it is on brown paper.
✳ Now they should colour the animal brown with either home-made brown paint, school paint or brown pastels. If they are using their own brushes, they won't be able to wash them, so tell them to just dip the brush in the earth paint; it will come out patchy, which will look quite authentic.
✳ Details such as cracks on the wall, fur or markings on the animals, etc can be added last.

Egyptian painting

SKILL

Time
2 hours
Link
History
Resources
Newspaper to cover tables
Per pair of children:
Powder paint or ready-mixed:
ultramarine (brilliant blue), white,
black, vermilion, lemon yellow
Gold ready-mixed paint
1 water pot
1 palette
For each child:
1 fine long-handled brush
1 fine watercolour brush
A4 cartridge paper
Sketchbooks or paper
Test paper
For the teacher:
Access to images of Egyptian tomb
paintings
National Curriculum
1c, 4a,b,c, 5a,d

Rita Roberts, Year 6

Introduction

Today you are going to do some paintings in the style and colours of the ancient Egyptians. They used particular colours because only some colours had been invented in paint form at that time. They created six new colours and a new kind of white, and you will also be using gold as gold is a colour that they used a lot of in their jewellery, masks and sculptures.

Practical activity

❋ Read children the section on Egyptian painting on page 91 and the BC section of the colour timeline on page 93.

❋ Show some images of tomb paintings and discuss the way the human figure is portrayed.

❋ Ask children to try to stand in the same way the figures stand, with the head facing to the side, shoulders to the front and feet both facing the same way. They will find it very hard to balance and will realize how unnatural the pose is.

❋ Tell the children they are going to try to draw a put-together figure – the head of one person, the shoulders of another and so on.

❋ Ask one child to pose for the profile of the head and face.

❋ Tell the children to draw one eye as seen from the side.

❋ Next ask another child to pose, facing the class, for the shoulders and body.

❋ The last model should stand sideways, with one leg in front of the other and feet facing the same way.

❋ Now tell them to draw a similar figure on their paper and add ancient Egyptian clothes and a collar and headdress.

❋ They should now paint the drawing using only the colours available to the Egyptian artists:
  • Ultramarine (to be blue frit)
  • White
  • Vermilion (to be cinnabar)
  • Orange
  • Lemon yellow
  • A yellow-brown (ochre)
  • Bright green (malachite)
  • Brown (umber)
  • Black

❋ Lastly they could paint the background gold, just for effect.

Medieval art: Illuminated letters

SKILL

Time
2 hours

Link
RE/History

Resources
Newspaper to cover tables

Per pair of children:
Powder paint or ready-mixed:
• crimson + vermilion red
• cyan + brilliant blue
• brilliant + lemon yellow
(or a tin of watercolours)
Gold ready-mixed paint
1 water pot
1 palette

For each child:
Watercolour brushes, fine and
medium sizes
A4 cartridge paper
Sketchbooks or paper
Test paper
1 fine-line black pen

For the teacher:
Access to images of illuminated
manuscripts

National Curriculum
1c, 4a,b,c, 5a,d

Nicky Loat, Year 5 (illuminated letter L)

Introduction
Today you are going to design and paint your own illuminated letters. (Read the section on European illuminated manuscripts on page 91.)

Practical activity
* Show the children the images of the illuminated lettering and explain that the scene depicted inside or around the letter often related to the content of the paragraph.
* Ask them to choose the first letter of one of their names and ask them to design a letter in their sketchbooks and decorate the letter itself. If they want to, they can place some images about themselves in the background, or take ideas from illuminated letters that they have been shown, or they could simply use patterns and shapes they like.
* Remind them that the monks would have

taken weeks, maybe months, over one tiny painting, and ask them to take time and trouble with their designs.
* When they have completed the design, it could be photocopied to save the children doing it again, or they could copy it onto white paper.
* Next, tell them to paint it in using bright, jewel-like colours.
* Explain to the children that the monks would have considered their art to be 'to the glory of their God' and so would want to do their very best work as part of their worship.
* Remind them that the blue and gold were incredibly expensive and that the monks would have used them very carefully and sparingly.
* When the painting is dry, children could go over the outlines with a black fine-line pen.

Using works of art

Hettie Pearson, Year 6 (in the style of Andy Warhol)

Artists and art movements

Children gain confidence through the ability to handle and control a substance as complex as paint, and by being able to express and communicate ideas through painting. Learning about the way artists, past and present, have used paint can extend the range of possibilities for children in their knowledge and in their thinking.

Studying the works of an artist, whether famous or relatively unknown, is often an excellent way of trying out the techniques favoured by various art movements.

It is essential to have access to a good supply of materials, such as prints of paintings by your chosen artists. These do not have to be expensive items – they can be old calendars, cut up and laminated, birthday or Christmas cards, or even old art books which are too tatty to use in the library, cut up and laminated.

Shops that sell remaindered books are an excellent source of art books, but be careful to go through them and make sure there are no unsuitable images. I do not mean nudes, as these are part of classical art history and children need to get used to seeing these without sniggering (more about this later), but there can be really unsuitable images, including those that are violent, disturbing or erotic. For example, check before you consider using any books on Klimt, because of his erotic drawings.

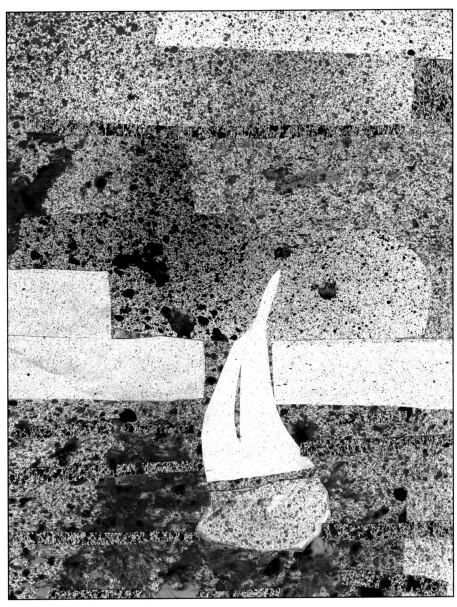

Year 6 pupil (in the style of Georges Seurat)

The National Gallery's website has a wonderful zoom facility whereby you can zoom in on any area of the picture and see it in detail. Try it with Fra Filippo Lippi's Annunciation and you can even see the tiny slit in the skirts of the stomach area where the spirit of God is about to enter. Or, try Canaletto's 'Stonemason's yard', where you can zoom in and show the children where the fallen toddler is weeing himself in surprise. They will like that!

Particularly useful artists to use with children

John Constable (English, 1776–1837)
Used in Watercolours (page 77)

Constable is probably England's most famous landscape painter. He painted many rural scenes from his home area of Suffolk. 'I should paint my own places best' he is known to have said. His paintings are considered to be romantic, which means they tend to represent a perfect or idyllic image. He is a good artist to use when trying to demonstrate to children how to create the illusion of distance in a painting.

Paul Klee (Swiss, 1879–1940)
Used in Colour theory (page 63)
Used in Watercolours (page 75)

Paul Klee is a wonderful artist to use with children as his work has a childlike quality. He was fascinated with children's artwork and children relate well to this quality, which makes his work accessible to them and non-threatening.

Klee worked on colour mixing in a progressive series of works as part of his teaching at the Bauhaus design school in West Germany. Many of his experiments were carried out in the form of beautiful small watercolours, painted in many overlapping layers of transparent colour, mostly based on just two colours. Many of his paintings show a range of colours juxtaposed, and these are excellent for children to look at when learning about colour mixing or colour relationships.

Henri Rousseau (French, 1844–1910)
Rousseau is particularly useful to use if children have been studying wild animals, green colour mixing or jungles. Children might like to know that he never went to the jungle or ever saw any wild animals or jungle plants, except in the zoological gardens in Paris. His style is slightly naive, which makes it easy for children to relate to.

Georges Seurat (French, 1859–1891)
Used in Using works of art (pages 107–108)

Seurat was born in Paris to wealthy parents, his mother would often take him for walks in the parks of Paris, and some of his most famous paintings are of parks. He was very shy and quiet and when he died, at the age of 31, his parents burnt all his papers, so very little is known about his life.

Seurat's experimentation with colour – and in particular his idea that the colours could be painted separately in small dots or dashes and the eye of the viewer would do the colour mixing – makes him an interesting artist to work with when children are studying either the art movement to which he belonged ('Pointillism') or colour mixing and colour theory.

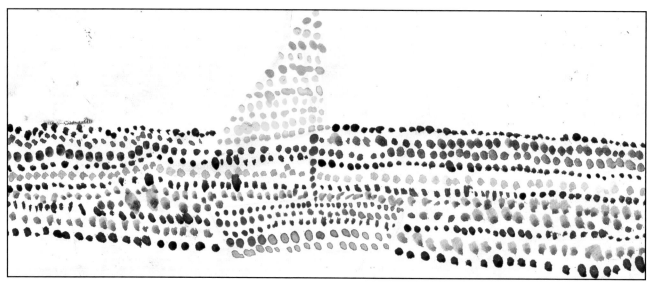

Aran Goldsmith, Year 5 (in the style of Seurat)

Georgia O'Keeffe (American, 1887–1986)
Georgia O'Keeffe's large dramatic paintings of flowers, often painted in single colours or just two colours, are ideal for children to look at when they are painting for any reason in a restricted palette (perhaps because they are investigating a range of one colour or are experimenting with simple colour mixing). Her paintings have tremendous mood and impact.

Claude Monet (French, 1840–1926)
Referred to in Oils (page 89)

Monet is an inspirational artist to tell children about. He would paint the same scene over and over again to capture it in different lights, times of day, weather conditions and seasons. Children can be shown his series of paintings of haystacks, water lilies or cathedrals, or of the famous gardens at Giverny – all paintings of the same scenes but in different colours. They can look at his works if they are studying subtle differences in colours, and also if they are concentrating on brush strokes. It is easy for them to see these in many of his paintings.

Vincent Van Gogh (Dutch, 1853–1890)
Referred to in Oils (page 89)
Used in Using works of art (page 106)
Used in Other techniques and media (page 111)

Van Gogh's vigorous brush marks are clear for children to see. They can see the passion and mood of his paintings and discuss his vivid use of colour. Children are often interested to hear that Van Gogh was a late starter who didn't begin drawing until he was 26 and wasn't very good to start with. They might also like to hear about his powerful emotions, to know that he tried to cut off his own ear, that he loved the colour yellow and that Don McLean's song 'Vincent' ('Starry starry night … ') was written about him. Films have also been made of his life story.

Franz Marc (German, 1880–1916)
Marc's use of strong bold colours, often combined with black, are dramatic and appealing to children – particularly his paintings of animals.

Marc Chagall (Russian, 1887–1985)
Chagall painted many dream-like paintings which feature stories, family scenes such as weddings and parties, and other aspects of his life in Russia. The slightly childlike folk quality of many of his pictures appeals to children and is a good source for paintings on a dream theme.

Gustav Klimt (Austrian, 1862–1918)
Klimt's work is a glorious mixture of colours, patterns and textures. He uses gold, golden yellows and brilliant jewel-like colours in his works, and the subject matter is often heavy with symbolism. While a lot of his works are semi-erotic (check for this before you use any books on his work), there are a number of works that are inspirational for children to work from, eg 'The tree of life', 'Portrait of Adele Bloche-Bauer 1' and his 'Apple tree', 'Poppy field' and 'Sunflower'.

Wassily Kandinsky (Russian, 1866–1944)
Used in Colour theory (page 63)

Kandinsky's use of brilliant colours and often non-figurative compositions make him an excellent artist to use with even very young children, especially when they are just concentrating on working in colour. His work is distinctive and children can easily recognize it. He worked in a group of artists in a movement called 'The Blue Rider', which included Paul Klee, Franz Marc and August Macke, all of whom are wonderful artists to use with children. He was possibly the first 'abstract' artist.

Robert Delauney (French, 1885–1941)
Delauney was a pioneer of abstract art who painted some compositions which were of pure colour in concentric circles. These are a good starting-point for children when mixing and painting colours as the composition is not daunting, and you can explain to the children that he was experimenting with different colour combinations.

Friedrich Hundertwasser (Austrian, 1928–2000)
Hundertwasser's work is extraordinary; he was an architect as well as a painter. It is very difficult to describe his work, as his paintings are full of brilliant colours and lines and often include houses in the compositions. He, rather like the Catalan architect Gaudi, loved to soften the contours of buildings with curved edges and organic forms. Children respond well to his colourful and unusual paintings and they are a good vehicle for wax resist pictures because of his use of line and colour.

Pablo Picasso (Spanish, 1881–1973)
Used in Basic skills (page 28)

Picasso is an inspirational artist to use with children because of the enormous range of his work, which includes not only painting but also ceramics, sculpture, collage and graphics. They need to understand that he could draw superbly by the age of 15 and spent the rest of his life experimenting and pushing artistic boundaries. One of the aspects of Picasso that is so inspiring is the sheer force of his creativity and the fact that he was still trying new styles and ideas in his 90s.

Joseph Turner (British, 1775–1851)
Turner is probably one of Britain's best-known painters, along with Constable. Turner was a master at painting light and the energy of the elements. Children might like to hear that the inspiration for a painting called 'Snow storm' arose when he was tied to the mast of a boat for four hours during a terrible storm, and he later painted this picture based on his experience. He is an excellent artist for children to study when they are using watercolours and are trying to get a feeling of lightness and brightness, particularly in skies.

Amadeo Modigliani (Italian, 1884–1920)
Used in Colour mixing (page 50)

Modigliani is probably the archetypal 'bohemian' artist who loved, lived and drank well but not wisely. He was passionate, romantic, good-looking and died young. He was also a brilliant artist. His work is very distinctive as his portraits tend to have elongated faces and necks. He was much influenced by African sculptures and masks. Children might like to hear that, in a fit of passion and depression, he threw many of his sculptures in the river Seine in Paris.

Piet Mondrian (Dutch, 1872–1944)
A lot (but not all) of Mondrian's works are easily recognizable as he uses similar pictorial elements in them: the straight line, the horizontal line, the primary colours, red, yellow and blue and the non-colours black, grey and white. For this reason, he is excellent to use as a starting-point for work on learning the primary colours. Simple Mondrian-like paintings are easily achievable by even quite young children. This work can be combined with maths, in the study of right angles, rectangles and squares. He was part of an art group known as 'De Stijl'.

Jackson Pollock (American, 1912–1956)
Jackson Pollock was a pioneer of an art movement called 'Action painting'; he would throw, spray, trickle or splatter the paint on top of the surface of the canvas layer upon layer, building up a highly patterned and textured surface. He would even ride a bike over it. The action involved in the making of the painting was as important as the look of the final artwork. Children will enjoy using some of his techniques: different colours of paint can be dribbled from squeezy bottles onto the paper and toy cars can be run through the paint. This works as well with very young children as it does with older ones.

Maurice de Vlaminck (born in France, 1876–1958)
Used in Acrylics (page 83)
Referred to in Oils (page 89)

Vlaminck first earned his living as a violinist and professional cyclist. However, even as a child, he had an irresistible urge to paint. Vlaminck, with his fellow painter André Derain, were the leaders in an art movement known as the Fauves (wild animals) partly because they painted in intense colours, thick paint, and their paintings showed tremendous drama and movement.

Some art movements of the 19th and 20th century
Here are some art movements that you might want to refer to at some point with your pupils. Many of them are mentioned at some point in this book.

Fauves (based in Paris in the 1900s)
The Fauves means wild animals, which was partly because they painted in intense colours, thick paint, and their paintings showed tremendous drama and movement.

Artists include André Derain, Maurice de Vlaminck and Henri Matisse.

Pre-Raphaelites (mainly French and British, 1848 onwards)
They painted very realistically, often depicting romantic scenes from medieval England, from Shakespeare, legends and poems. Children may enjoy hearing the stories behind the paintings: the Arthurian legends or 'The Lady of Shalott'. The Pre-Raphaelites are much scorned by art snobs.

Impressionists (Europe, 1860s onwards)
The Impressionists, as the name suggests, were interested in capturing an impression – a fleeting moment of light and atmosphere. They were revolutionary at the time in showing loose brush marks and not tight realism, and their paintings met with violent negative responses from the established art world. The most famous artists involved in the movement were Monet, Renoir, Manet, Sisley, Degas and Cézanne.

Post-Impressionists (Dutch and French,1880s)

Some artists turned away from the ideas of the Impressionists and went their own way. The most famous of these were Paul Gauguin and Vincent Van Gogh, two artists who had a turbulent friendship and greatly influenced each other's work.

Pointillism (2nd half of 19th century)

Pointillism is a style of painting in which small distinct dots of colour create the impression of a wide selection of other colours. The colour mixing is done in the eye and mind of the viewer. Pointillism was figurative rather than abstract. The most famous painter in this movement was Georges Seurat.

Cubism (Europe, end of 19th century)

This movement abandoned traditional methods, perspective and vision, portraying a subject from several viewpoints, searching for and emphasizing its geometric forms. Cézanne was the first cubist and he inspired and influenced other artists such as Picasso and Braque.

Abstract painting (Europe, end of 19th century onwards)

This is generally considered to be non-representational art, ie it does not attempt to represent nature or any recognizable subject matter. Kandinsky was the artist who made the first step towards complete abstraction.

Another sub-group of artists who could also be called abstract artists were known as 'De Stijl', a movement that was formed in Holland in 1917. Their paintings contained mainly horizontal and vertical lines, and the most famous exponent was Mondrian.

Surrealism (Europe, 1923 onwards)

This was an art movement which stressed the importance of the irrational and the subconscious. Surrealist paintings are often quite strange and can be disturbing to children. The most famous exponent is the Spanish artist Salvador Dali.

Dada (Switzerland, 1914)

The Dadaists were a group of artists who wanted to produce art that shocked people, just as the First World War, which was then starting, was shocking. The name Dada was chosen at random, but it is in fact a French word for a child's rocking horse. The Dada artists were very anti-art, and had their own ideas of art that were not the same as those of the rest of society. Marcel Duchamp was an artist working in this movement. He liked to take ready-made objects and exhibit them as art in galleries. His most famous work in this genre, the children might like to hear, was a urinal.

Action painting (USA, 1950s)

These paintings were sometimes painted using the hands directly on the canvas, or by throwing or dribbling the paint onto the canvas. The artwork was as much about the actual movement and the physical involvement of the artist as it was about the way the painting looked. Children generally thoroughly enjoy having a go at this!

Pop art (USA, 1960s)

Used in Colour mixing (page 52)

In the 1960s, the music of the Beatles was heard throughout the world. Art could also become 'pop' like music. Pop artists welcomed the images we see today, such as cans of Coke, advertisements and comic books. The artists working in this movement used the mass production of their age to produce their work, which often includes repeated images. These reflect the posters and rows of products that could be found on supermarket shelves (supermarkets themselves were new in the 1960s) . Iconic images from films and television were often taken and altered. Andy Warhol was one of the artists working in this style.

'Op' art (Britain, 1960s)

Op art is short for 'optical art'. The artists working in this movement were interested in deceiving the eye of the viewer in different ways, creating optical illusions. Work was often in black and white and very sharp and well defined. The British artist Bridget Riley was a major exponent of op art, but she also worked in dazzling colours that contrasted and created strong after-images in complementary colours. Her research was highly mathematical and exact, and the illusions she created were not there by chance.

Naïve and Primitive artists

This is not an art movement but a style or type of art. It is often used to describe the work of artists who have received no formal training in art, who have come to painting relatively late in life, or who use aspects of folk art extensively or have a childlike quality. Rousseau and Lowry could be described as having Naïve qualities.

Questioning that will enhance children's responses to and understanding of works of art

What do children gain from looking at art?

Children gain two huge advantages from looking at art. The first is that they learn about their heritage as artists – whether that heritage is national or worldwide. For this, they need to see as wide a variety of paintings as possible, so that their working definitions are flexible and generous.

The second gain is to children's own artwork and working methods. Children who have examined other art forms will work with greater technique (provided they have been led to consider how the work was done) and a greater openness about what their painting materials can do. Hopefully, they will also have been inspired by the passion and interest communicated by the teacher. With careful choice of artworks and skilful questioning, children can be led, open-eyed and open-hearted, into the world of the visual arts.

How to access works of art

If the teacher has access to an interactive whiteboard, and most classrooms do have them now, it is relatively easy to download large-scale images of works of art so that children may look at the image at the same time and share their responses. The easiest way is to use the Google search engine (www.google.co.uk) and click on 'Images'. In the search box, enter the image or artist you want and this will bring up a selection of images to choose from.

If an interactive whiteboard is not an option (perhaps work is taking place in an art room where there is no board, or a board is not available for whatever reason), then the school will need to build up a collection of reproductions of works of art, from postcard-sized reproductions to large posters. If the school has contact with a local artist who is able to lend or come and show some of their work, then this opportunity should be exploited. To hear an artist talk about their work is a powerful experience, as is hearing background information about art from an art expert.

In the absence of artists or art experts, however, there are many different ways to encourage children to respond to a work of art, to draw them in and to involve them. The teacher, and the children, can talk about the painting.

What to say and what to ask

Questions the teacher might ask break down into four areas:

* Description: what do you see?
* Analysis: how are things put together?
* Interpretation: what is the artist trying to say?
* Judgement: what do you think of it?

It is probably best to ask children what they see, know and think before we tell them what we see, know and think, although it is tempting to talk first when we are sharing a picture we know and to which we have a strong response ourselves. Between the whole class, they may spot more than we think they will. If we have some information and questions ready, we can fill the gaps and extend the understanding.

Possible questions might include:

Opening questions
* What do you see?
* What is going on in the picture?
* Do you think there is a story behind it?
* What is the mood of the picture?
* What time of year, day and season do you think it is?
* Do you think it was painted long ago, a while ago, or quite recently?
* Is it realistic (lifelike)?

Colour
* Is the painting bright and colourful?
* Are the colours mostly pale/all in one colour/dark?
* Is there one colour that stands out?
* Why is this?
* Is there a dominant colour?
* Does that colour help the mood?
* Has the artist used hot/cold/complementary/harmonious/earth colours?
* How does this help to convey the feeling?
* What (kinds of) colours have been used?

* Are the colours 'real life colours'?
* Why is the sky that colour?
* Is it that colour to help create an atmosphere?

Portraits
* Do you know, or have you heard of, the person in the painting?
* Do you think they would have liked it?
* How many people are in the picture?
* What do you think the person is thinking/ feeling?
* What might they say if they could speak to you?
* Can you see any groups of people in the picture?
* What are they doing?
* Why do you think that artist has put them in?
* Describe the clothes they are wearing.
* Which one would you like/not like to be?

General
* Where do you think the light is coming from?
* What might have happened before/after this moment?
* Can you see the artist's brush strokes?
* How do you think the artist has done that?
* Why do you think they chose this subject?
* What has the artist used (watercolour, oil paint, etc)?
* Why do you think they chose to use (whatever medium it is)?
* What shapes can you find?
* Would you buy this picture?
* Is there anything in the painting that might be symbolic?
* Why do you think this picture was painted?

* How has the (specific things such as clouds, hair, hills, etc) been painted?
* How does this picture make you feel?
* What do you think of it?
* If you had painted it, is there anything you would have changed?
* What do you think the artist was feeling when they painted this?
* How has the artist made things look far away/close to?
* How did the artist create the mood of the painting?
* Do you think they enjoyed painting it?
* Why do you think that?
* Does the painting remind you of the work of another artist?
* Have you seen the painting before? If so, where?
* Is it a successful painting? Why do you think that? Who thinks something different?
* Where was the painting made to be seen – a private house, a church, a gallery, or some other public place?

Once the first few questions start and children make different responses, it is quite easy to extend this by asking children if they agree or disagree with what someone else has said.

It is important, when the children are discussing their own responses to a work of art, that they understand they are entitled to have an opinion that is different from those of others. They should know that the artist may have wanted people to look at their work and have different responses. Children must feel free to make comment without fear of censure from other children.

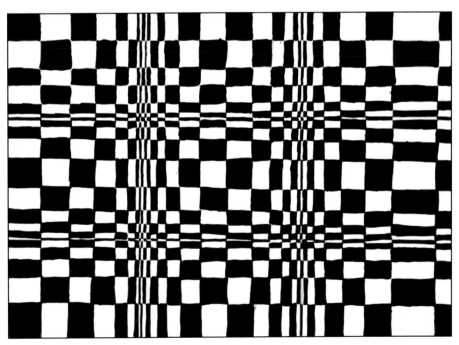

Ebony Thorne, Year 6 (in the style of Bridget Riley)

SKILL Using a painting by Van Gogh

Time
3 hours and possibly more than one session

Resources
Newspaper to cover tables

Per pair of children:
Powder paint or ready-mixed colours:
- 2 reds: vermilion and crimson
- 2 blues: brilliant blue and cyan
- 2 yellows: brilliant and lemon yellow
1 water pot
1 palette

For each child:
1 fine and 1 medium long-handled brush
A3 cartridge paper
Test papers

For the teacher:
Access to a copy of Van Gogh's painting 'Starry Night' or any one of his paintings that clearly show brush marks
Information about Van Gogh on page 101.

National Curriculum
2a, 4a,c, 5a

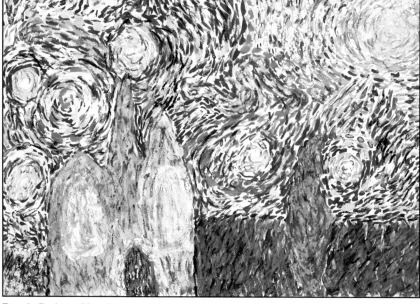

Emmie Perham, Year 6

Introduction
If you look at the work of Vincent Van Gogh, two things really stand out: one is that you ca clearly see his brushstrokes and the other is a strong sense of movement and energy. Today you are going paint your own version of his painting 'Starry night' and try to use similar brush marks and get a feeling of movement and energy into your paintings.

Practical activity
※ Show the children the painting and discuss what can be seen.
※ Tell them that they can change the time of day or the season or the weather or even the composition of the painting if they want to, but to use the painting as a starting point. Explain that what you will be looking for in their paintings is separate brush strokes and a feeling of movement.
※ Point out that the sense of movement might be achieved by making sure that there is a consistent direction to their brush strokes.

※ Tell the children that they can build the painting up in layers, if the layer below is dry and they use a light touch so as not to disturb the under-layer of paint (unless they are working in acrylics).
※ Children should use a thin mixture of pale blue paint (pale blue will disappear when it is painted over) and a fine brush to map out their basic composition.
※ Tell them to take one area at a time and decide which two or three shades of colour will be needed for that area. For example, a tree might be three different greens or the sun might be three shades of yellow and oranges.
※ Then they should decide on a direction for the brush strokes and paint in that area, making sure the brush strokes all follow in that direction.
※ Ask them not to use too much or too thick paint on the brush, and to aim for quick, light flicks of the brush.
※ They should continue to build up the painting in this way an area at a time.
※ When it is dry, they could try to view it as a whole and make whatever adjustments they want to.
※ They should continue to work on it, adding other colours and deepening the tones to make the picture stronger.

SKILL Using a painting by Seurat (spatter technique: session 1)

Time
2 hours

Resources
Newspaper to cover tables
Some old washing-up brushes, nail brushes or toothbrushes
A few old combs
Paper plates for the paints

Per small group of children:
Ready-mixed colours:
- 2 reds: vermilion and crimson
- 2 blues: brilliant blue and cyan
- 2 yellows: brilliant and lemon yellow
1 water pots
Several water pots to mix paint in

For each child:
2 or 3 sheets of any A3 paper
Protective clothing (including goggles if you want to play safe)

For the teacher:
Access to a copy of one of Seurat's paintings, painted in tiny dots of colour
Information about Seurat on page 100 and Pointillism on page 103

National Curriculum
2a, 4a,c, 5a

Bethany Green, Year 6

Note
You will need another activity for the rest of the class while a few at a time are spattering paint, unless you have an adult to assist. They could do a miniature dot painting using fine brushes.

Introduction
If you look at the work of Seurat, you will see that it is made up of a series of little dots of different colours. Seurat was part of an art movement called the Pointillists and you are going to try to create a picture in a similar way to him.

Practical activity
※ Read the information to the children about Seurat and the Pointillists (pages 100 and 103).
※ Explain to the children that they are not going to paint a big picture using lots of little dots of paint as that will take a very long time, but they will be using the same system of dots of different colours that the eye will blend when viewed from a distance.

※ Working with no more than three or four children at a time, tell them to:
  - Study the painting and mix up two colours that they think will blend to make a third they can see in the painting. For example, if the colour they want is purple, tell them to mix up some brilliant blue and some crimson.
  - Tip some of each colour onto separate plates.
  - Dip a toothbrush in one of the paints, hold the brush over the paper (trying not to drip on the paper, though this can be difficult).
  - Pull the bristles back towards themselves, using an old comb or their fingers aiming the bristles at the paper, and release them.
  - As they release the bristles, the paint should splatter all over the paper (and probably themselves as well if they have pointed the bristles in the wrong way).
  - Repeat this with the second colour on the same piece of paper. They should do several sheets of spattered paper in their two colours.
※ The next group should choose another two colours to combine and repeat the process.
※ Continue until there are enough sheets of spattered coloured paper for the whole class to cut up when they are dry.

Using a painting by Seurat (spattered paper: session 2)

SKILL

Time
3 hours – could be over several sessions

Resources
Glue sticks
Scissors

Per group or table of children:
One of each colour of the spattered papers

For each child:
1 piece of A4 paper
1 A3 enlarged photocopy of one of Seurat's paintings

For the teacher:
Access to a copy of one of Seurat's paintings, painted in tiny dots of colour; 'Sunday afternoon on the Isle of the Grand Jatte' and 'The Bathers' are good examples

National Curriculum
2a, 4a,c, 5a

Tamsin Cook, Year 6

Introduction
If you look at the work of Seurat, you will see that it is made up of a series of little dots of different colours. Seurat was part of an art movement called the Pointillists and you are going to try to create a picture in a similar way to him.

Practical activity
✳ Re-read the information about Seurat and the Pointillists to the children (pages 100 and 103).
✳ Show them the Seurat paintings they will be using. Discuss these.
✳ Ask the children to choose an area of the painting that they like and to draw a rectangle around it.
✳ Next tell them to copy this section, simplifying it and enlarging it up to A4 size (less able children may need to have theirs enlarged on the photocopier).
✳ The children should look at the spattered papers in front of them and decide which colours would be appropriate for the background; this could be two different colours to represent the horizon or the bank of the river. They should cut out and glue down this piece or pieces onto their A4 paper.

✳ Now they should look at the spattered papers in front of them and decide which colours would be appropriate for which sections of their picture. The colours do not need to be the same as in the picture, but they should be spattered in two colours of paint.
✳ Next, children should follow this sequence for each separate area of their picture.
  1. Cut out one section of their drawn picture.
  2. Lay it over the coloured paper they have chosen for that area.
  3. Draw around it.
  4. Cut it out.
  5. Stick it down, or lay it ready for sticking, on the background.
✳ They should repeat this sequence until they have a collaged version of their original section of Seurat's painting.
✳ They could frame the edges of the picture using spattered colours that are complementary to the inside area, as Seurat did.
✳ Lastly, the children should view their paintings from a distance to see if the spots and dots of colour seem to have merged.

Other techniques and media

Joyce Horridge, Year 6

Other methods of applying paint

It is important to point out that brushes are not the only method of applying paint to a surface. Most children enjoy inventing and making their own painting implements. An example of this is in a lesson on page 94 in the History of painting chapter. Children should have the opportunity to experiment with such things as fingers, rags, strips of card, rollers and sponges.

Sponges, for example, offer endless opportunities for painting experiments. Rough textures and special effects can be achieved when paints of different consistencies are applied with natural or synthetic sponges of various degrees of coarseness.

Cotton buds are useful as they are easy to hold and are absorbent, and they keep their shape well. They are especially useful for painting small, precise areas, such as petals and stamens of flowers, or for painting in the style of the Pointillists or Aborigine dot pictures.

Fur fabric can be used to apply paint, for example to create a grassy effect.

Single prints can be made from paintings while the paint is still wet by placing a sheet of paper on the top of the painting and peeling it off.

Marbles can be rolled in paint and then rolled across the paper.

Paint can also be:
* Dropped or dripped onto the paper
* Thrown on as in action painting (if you are very brave, have a large space to work in and are prepared for the ensuing mess)
* Splattered on by pulling back the bristle of a stiff brush, such as a toothbrush or a washing-up brush
* Sprayed on with a diffuser or an aerosol can
* Blown in different directions along the page through a straw (thin paint or ink)
* Sprinkled onto a wet surface as dry powder
* Scraped with a variety of implements.

Texture

Fabric can be pressed into wet paint to create a texture in a painting.

Thick paint can be applied with a plastic or palette knife to create a rough, uneven texture which is called 'impasto'.

Substances can be added to paint to make it thicker or textured, including PVA, sawdust, salt, starch, flour, icing sugar, crushed eggshells, sand or Polyfilla®.

Paint applied thickly can be scraped with twigs or the ends of brushes to make lines and marks in the paint.

Bits and pieces can be dropped onto thick wet paint such as dry grass, sand, sawdust, tissue paper, foil, thin fabric, netting or glitter.

Will Ayres, Year 5 (line and wash)

Line and wash

SKILL

Time
45 min

Links
History

Resources
Newspaper to cover tables

Per pair of children:
Pot of child-safe black ink, or black
Brusho® (see page 11)
Pot of water

For each child:
Pen with nib
A5 cartridge paper
Sketchbook or paper
1 fine-line black pen
1 medium watercolour brush

For the teacher:
Access to some pen drawings by Van
Gogh

National Curriculum
1a,c, 2a,b, 4a, 5a

Thomas Corras, Year 5

Note
If using black ink, rather than black Brusho®, check
the label to make sure it is safe to use with children.
This technique works in a similar way with charcoal
and water.

Introduction
*Line and wash is a drawing and painting technique that is
quite old. Ink has been used in many parts of the world for
well over 2,000 years. The ancient Egyptians, Greeks, and
Romans used pens made from reeds. The Romans also made
pens out of bronze, some of which had nibs shaped very
much like the ones we use today. Feather quills were used
in Europe in the seventh century. In fact the Italian word for
feather is 'penna' which is where we get the word pen. Quill
pens remained the most popular form of nib until the steel
nib was invented in America in the 19th century. The penknife
is called a penknife because it was a small pocket knife that
was used to cut off the end of a feather to make a pen. You
are going to try out using pens with nibs, and then adding a
thin wash of ink over the drawings to create tones.*

Practical activity
❋ Show the children the pen drawings by Van
Gogh and draw their attention to all the
different marks he made with his pen.

❋ The children should go outside and draw
trees in their sketchbooks with fine-line black
pens. If they cannot go outside, they will
have to work from photographs and books.

❋ Now ask the children to experiment with
making lines and marks in their sketchbooks
with the pens dipped in black ink. There will
be a lot of blots, so they will have to practise
stroking the nib on the side of the pot to
remove excess ink and transferring the pen
to the paper carefully.

❋ When they have gained some control (it is
very difficult) over the pen and ink, they should
draw some trees on their cartridge paper.

❋ They could add a horizon or some hills in the
background and shrubs, plants and grass
textures in the foreground.

❋ The children should dip their brushes in the
water and float the water gently over the
parts of the trees that would have leaves,
over the foreground and shrubs. The ink
should move a little and a soft, pale grey
wash should be created.

❋ Deeper tones of this can be made by adding
a little ink to the water to make a mid-grey.
Touches of this can be used for darker
tones on the trees, in the skies for clouds or
foreground for shadows.

❋ Allow time for the children to experiment
with adding the washes. If there is time,
they could do further ink drawings and add
washes now they know what will happen and
the effects they can make

SKILL

Aborigine dreamtime pictures

Time
1 hour

Link
Other cultures

Resources
Newspaper to cover tables

Per pair of children
Black, white, red, orange, yellow and
brown ready-mixed paint
1 palette
Several cotton buds in each colour

For each child:
A3 brown sugar paper
Pencil
Sketchbook

For the teacher:
Access to some Aborigine dot pictures
showing animals
Pictures of Australian animals

National Curriculum
1c, 2a,b,c, 4a,c, 5a

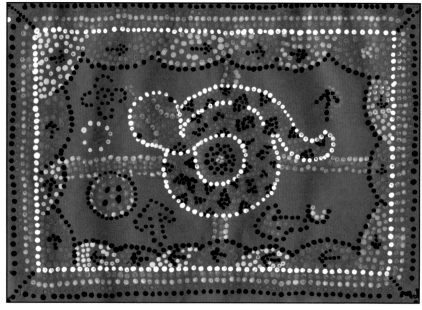

Year 6 pupil

Introduction

*The Aborigine people of Australia use many different symbols
in their pictures. Circles inside other circles mean campsites,
water holes or resting places, several lines in a row mean
people travelling or pathways, and wavy lines mean running
water or smoke. Dots mean lots of different things like rain,
eggs, ants and other things. They also create whole pictures
out of dots of different colours, which is what you will be
doing. They use natural materials found in the areas where
they live to make their colours; these are what we would call
earth colours. You are going to use cotton wool buds dipped in
paint to print with.*

Practical activity

❋ Show the children the Aborigine artwork and
point out the way it has been built up out
of dots of colour and the animals they have
depicted.
❋ Children should look at the animal pictures,
then draw some animals in their sketchbooks
and decide on which they want to use in their
picture.

❋ Next, tell the children to draw a border
around the inside of the paper and then a
simplified version of their chosen animal in
the centre.
❋ Now children should print dots of white
around the outline of the animal to define it.
❋ Tell them to print no more than five or six
dots before they re-dip the cotton bud into
the paint again (see Potential pitfall below).
❋ Next, children should concentrate on the
animal and fill it in with patterns appropriate
to the animal's skin or fur.
❋ The animal can then be connected to the
border with double printed dotty lines to
represent the animal's travels.
❋ Other symbols could be printed in the centre
area.
❋ Lastly, the border can be printed in a
repeating colour pattern.
❋ If the children have time (and patience), they
could fill in all the spaces left in contrasting
colours.

Potential pitfall

Children tend to try to print too many dots before
re dipping their buds into the paint, the result of
this is that the dots get paler and paler as the
paint runs out, which spoils the effectiveness of
the printing.

SKILL	# Blow paintings

Time
1 hour

Resources
Newspaper to cover tables

Per pair of children:
Black Brusho® in a pot (see page 11)

For each child:
A4 white paper
A plastic straw
1 medium paintbrush
Protective clothing

For the teacher:
Paper and a straw to demonstrate

National Curriculum
2a,b, 4a, 5a

Kelly White, Year 5

Note
If children blow too hard and for too long at a time, they may feel dizzy.

Introduction
You are going to try creating some trees, plants and creatures by blowing thin paint along the paper with a straw. You cannot ever be quite sure which way the paint will go, so the end results can be not what you planned. You have to make the best of what happens!

Practical activity
❋ Demonstrate the technique to children by showing the children how to:
  1. Pour a little Brusho® onto the paper.
  2. Place the straw directly above the Brusho®.
  3. Blow very hard down on it.
  4. Chase the paint outwards to make spiky lines.
❋ Explain that they can drop a little more Brusho® on if they want to and continue blowing.
❋ Tell the children to have a go at this.
❋ Explain that they can also crouch down level with the paper and blow horizontally along the surface.

❋ Also tell them that they can chase one Brusho® droplet along in any direction, and if they blow from above, the colour will spread outwards.
❋ Remind them that the Brusho® seems to have a mind of its own.
❋ To make the tree, the children should:
  • Paint the trunk first.
  • Add extra Brusho® at the top of the trunk.
  • Blow the Brusho® upwards and outwards, adding extra black if they need to.
❋ This activity looks beautiful when done in more than one colour, and it lends itself to creating fantasy creatures. Features, limbs, hair, etc can be added later with a fine pen.

Potential pitfall
Children must not suck instead of blow. This might seem obvious, but someone in the class is bound to try it. If Indian ink is being used (not advised), it could be toxic, so check the label.

Assessment

Jay Jury, Year 6

Assessment of painting

I am tempted to start this section with the subtitle 'If you really must'! However, if you must, for whatever reason, here are a few pointers.

* You could keep one good example of some work at the end of a unit (say, colour mixing) and put it in a child's record of achievement with comments by both you and the child
* You could make a note of aspects of painting where a child has excelled or struggled
* You could make a note about attitude and confidence in relation to painting
* You could set each child some simple targets at the end of the first term, for example:
  * Work more independently
  * Use the space on the paper better
  * Mix more of your own colours
  * Don't rush to finish
  * Stop now and then and have a think how things are going
  * Don't give up too easily
  * Use less watery paint (ie mix it up more thickly)
  * Remember to use a brush that is right for the job.

  The children could add a target of their own and you could check the targets periodically to see if any of them have been met.
* You could photocopy the 'Experience and progression of skills' list for the appropriate year group, from page 9, and highlight in green the ones the children have covered or achieved and in red the ones they have struggled with. That would give you an idea of their weaknesses and strengths, and also what aspects you have covered and what they will need to do before the end of the year or in their next class.
* You could do this for the whole class or make three copies: one for each of a higher, middle and lower ability group. Or, if you are feeling very keen, you could do one for each child. These might be helpful when you come to write reports or on parents' evenings when you can't even think what the child looks like, let alone what they can or can't do in painting.
* You can always use lovely phrases like 'Seems to really enjoy painting' or 'Is beginning to develop an understanding of colour mixing'.
* Both phrases, of course mean nothing, but they sound positive and they don't pin you down. So, when the parent says, 'Actually he hates art,' you can reply, 'Well, perhaps that's because I'm such an old crab. But he seems to enjoy actually doing it!' Alternatively, if they say, 'She knows diddlysquat about painting,' you can reply, 'I only said she was beginning to develop an understanding … '

If the bird of Ofsted is due to land on your roof, don't worry. If you have used a range of painting media in different scales and genres, you will have done well and they will be happy. Just make sure that you display a few examples in a prominent place. Remember, if they can't find evidence of it, they may assume it is not happening. If the children have 'done well' then show it off!

Year 5 pupil (powder paint)

Pupils' self-assessment

Pupils' self-assessment

You should encourage self-assessment. This should really be happening during the lessons on a regular basis so that the children start to do it for themselves as they are working, without any prompting from you.

Suggest that the children look at their own work and think:

❋ Am I pleased with it? Why?
❋ Which bits work the best? Why?
❋ Which bits don't work so well? Why?
❋ What would I change if I did it again/worked on it later?
❋ If someone else had done this, what would I think?
❋ Have I used the space well?
❋ What is good about the colours I have used? What is not so good?
❋ What did I learn while I was doing this?
❋ Have I made the best use of the paints?
❋ Does my painting have a particular mood/feeling to it?

❋ How does it look from a distance?
❋ Have I done what I was asked, eg shown distance by the use of colour?

Allow time for reflection at the end of a session (if that is possible with the mountains of dirty palettes in teetering piles on the draining board).

Children could be asked if they have any comments to make on what they have done, or what others have done. If they are commenting on the work of their peers, encourage a climate of 'being a critical friend' so that their comments are kindly and constructive. You could start the ball rolling by asking one child to select a painting done by another child, hold it up (if it is not dripping wet) and say if they like it and why they think it is good. Then invite that child to choose the work of someone else to comment on. This will give you opportunities to bring out teaching points and reinforce the skills covered in that session.

Bibliography

Allen, Janet. *Exciting Things to Do with Colour*. Marks & Spencer Ltd

Barnes, Rob. *Art & Design and Topic Work*. Routledge

Clement, Robert and Page, Shirley. *Investigating and Making in Art*. Oliver Boyd

Cummings, Robert. *Just Imagine. Ideas in Painting*. Kestrel Books (Penguin)

Cummings, Robert. *Just Look. A Book about Paintings*. Viking (Penguin)

Fitzsimmons, Su. *Start with Art*. Stanley Thornes

Gombrich, E.H. *The Story of Art*. Phaidon Press

Hart, Tony. *Small Hands Big Ideas*. Guild Publishing, London

Hay, Penny. *Introducing Painting*. NES Arnold

Hayes, Colin. *The Complete Guide to Painting and Drawing, Techniques and Materials*. Phaidon.

Heslewood, Juliet. *The History of Western Painting*. Belitha Press.

King, Penny and Roundhill, Claire. *Portraits. Artists' Workshop*. A&C Black

King, Penny and Roundhill, Claire. *Animals. Artists' Workshop*. A&C Black

Kluge, Gisela. *Drawing, Painting, Printing*. Lutterworth Press

Meager, Nigel and Ashfield, Julie. *Teaching Art at Key Stage 2*. N.S.E.A.D.

Meager, Nigel. *Teaching Art at Key Stage 1*. N.S.E.A.D.

Pluckrose, Henry. *Paints*. Franklin Watts

Pluckrose, Henry. *The Art & Craft Book*. Evans Brothers Ltd, London

Powell, Gillian. *Painting and Sculpture*. Wayland

Richardson, Wendy and Jack. *Cities through the Eyes of Artists*. Heinemann

Solga, Kim. *Paint!* F&W Publications

Stocks, Sue. *Painting*. Wayland

Walters, Elizabeth and Harris, Anne. *Painting: A Young Artist's Guide*. Dorling Kindersley

Wenham, Martin. *Understanding Art: A Guide for Teachers*. Paul Chapman Publishing

Withey, David, Grosz, Jane and Fulton, Maggie. *Art: A Primary Teacher's Handbook*. Folens

Glossary

Abstract art
Pictures or sculptures which create an effect using line, tone, form, shape or colour but do not represent anything recognizable.

Acrylic paint
A water-based paint with a plastic binder.

Background
Anything which is behind the main image or which serves as a setting for an image. It can also mean the surface on which a painting is created.

Block paint
Paint that comes in compacted tablets, water-based and generally in basic bright colours.

Brusho®
Powdered watercolour paint that can be made up into a liquid.

Charcoal
Drawing stick made from charred wood.

Chiaroscuro
Italian for light/dark, meaning the use of light and shade in a painting.

Classical
Usually art that is either Greek or Roman or influenced by those styles.

Collage
A French term for describing artwork which includes many items stuck onto a surface.

Complementary colours
Pairs of colours that are opposite on the colour wheel and contrast strongly: blue/orange, yellow/purple, red/green.

Composition
The arrangement of colour, shape, line and so on in a picture.

Contrast
To stand out against something else.

Cubism
A movement in painting that abandoned traditional methods of modelling and perspective and portrayed a subject from several viewpoints at the same time and in simplified planes and shapes.

Connor Wisken, Year 6, oil on canvas. The big wave

Elements (of art)
Line, tone, texture. colour, form, shape and composition.

Earth colours
Pigments made from minerals such as ochre, sienna and umber – usually a mixture of browns, greens, blacks and greys.

Egg tempera
Paint using egg as the binder – usually the yolk, but sometimes the whole egg.

Expressionism
A style of art which exaggerates or distorts shape, line and colour to portray feelings.

Fauvism
Painting that uses colour to express emotion rather than reality. The Fauvists worked in the early 20th century to free painting from pictorial representation. Fauves means wild animals.

Ferrule
The metal holder of a brush, where the hair joins the handle.

Figurative
Art that depicts recognizable people, animals or objects; the opposite of abstract art.

Filbert
A conical-shaped brush.

Folk art
Decoration or objects made by people without formal training, who use traditional techniques, patterns, colours and forms.

Foreground
The lower area of a picture, or part of a scene which seems nearer to the viewer.

Form
A 3-D shape, or its representation in 2-D.

Fresco
A method of painting on a plaster wall while the plaster is still wet. The painting becomes part of the wall.

Futurism
Italian movement at its height from 1909–1914, which attempted to capture the beauty of speed and the machine.

Glaze
A thin layer of transparent or translucent paint applied over a picture to create subtle effects. Acrylic paint can be used in this way.

Gouache
A watercolour paint with white pigment added, making the colours more opaque.

Graffito
A method in which a line is produced by scratching through one painted surface to reveal another.

Ground
A substance applied to a support (canvas, board, paper) before the painting begins.

Hue (tint)
A colour or variety of a colour created by adding another colour.

Impasto
The thick application of paint.

Impressionism
A style of painting begun by a group of French artists at the end of the 19th century. They used bright colours, applied freely, to capture the effects of light.

Indian ink
A dense, black ink made from carbon.

Landscape
1. A scene which generally includes some of these elements: fields, hills, trees, grass, rivers, lakes, animals, skies, clouds and rural buildings.
2. In terms of paper or canvas, when the vertical sides are shorter than the horizontal sides.

Lapis lazuli
A blue stone from which the natural ultramarine pigment was once ground.

Media (medium, singular)
In painting, the material the artist uses to make the work of art. A set of materials.

Monochrome
Painted in one colour.

Mono print
A single print taken from a wet image, usually because only one 'take' is possible.

Mural
Painting on walls – implies on a large scale to fill the wall.

Ochre
Natural colours found in different types of earths used to make pigments.

Op art
Developed in the 1960s, paintings that used colour and pattern to create optical illusions.

Palette
1. Slab for mixing colours; can be plastic, china, wood, hardboard or paper.
2. A range of colours at an artist's disposal.

Patron
Someone who supports the arts by commissioning artists to work for him or her.

Perspective

A method of creating a sense of space and distance in a picture.

Pigment

Coloured material which gives the paint its colour, usually ground to a fine powder and mixed with a binder which holds it together and makes it stick to the support (paper, canvas, etc).

Pointillism

A painting technique using separate small dots which merge in the eye when viewed from a distance.

Polyptych

An altarpiece which is made up of several panels that are hinged and can close together.

Pop art

An art movement that was at its peak in the 1960s. The artists took images from the consumer society and popular culture such as television, packaging and advertising. They also used commercial methods of production such as printing.

Poster paint

Water-based, slightly opaque paint, similar to gouache.

Realism

The name given to paintings that try to show the world exactly as it is, even if that means painting unpleasant things.

Sable

An animal whose hair is used for fine soft brushes.

Scumble

To apply a thin, often broken layer of paint over a darker paint.

Sfumato

An Italian word meaning the gradual merging of colours with no sudden changes.

Shade

A colour, especially with regard to its depth or having been made darker by adding black.

Still life

A group of objects arranged together so that they can be drawn or painted. At one time, the objects depicted often had a deep significance.

Stipple

Brush marks made by using the vertical end of the brush, usually consisting of flattened dots.

Surrealism

An art movement which stressed the importance of the irrational and the subconscious. Surrealist paintings usually look strange or disturbing.

Technique

The process or practice that is used to obtain a particular effect.

Tempera

A paint that was originally made up from water, egg and colour. Chemical versions of it are still used.

Texture

Representation in a work of different surfaces, or actual variation in surface caused by the application of thick paint.

Tint

A change in a colour when a small amount of a different colour is added.

Tone

The lightness or darkness of a colour. Also used to describe the shades of grey between black and white.

Under-drawing

The drawing beneath a painting.

Under-painting

Layers of paint beneath the top layer of a painting, particularly those which show through glazes or semi-transparent top layers.

Value

In a colour, this means the strength of one colour from its lightest version to its deepest.

Vanishing point

The point or points at which parallel lines appear to meet on the horizon line.

Wash

A thin, diluted coat of paint applied over a broad area of the surface of a painting, often used as a base for painting.

Year 5 pupil

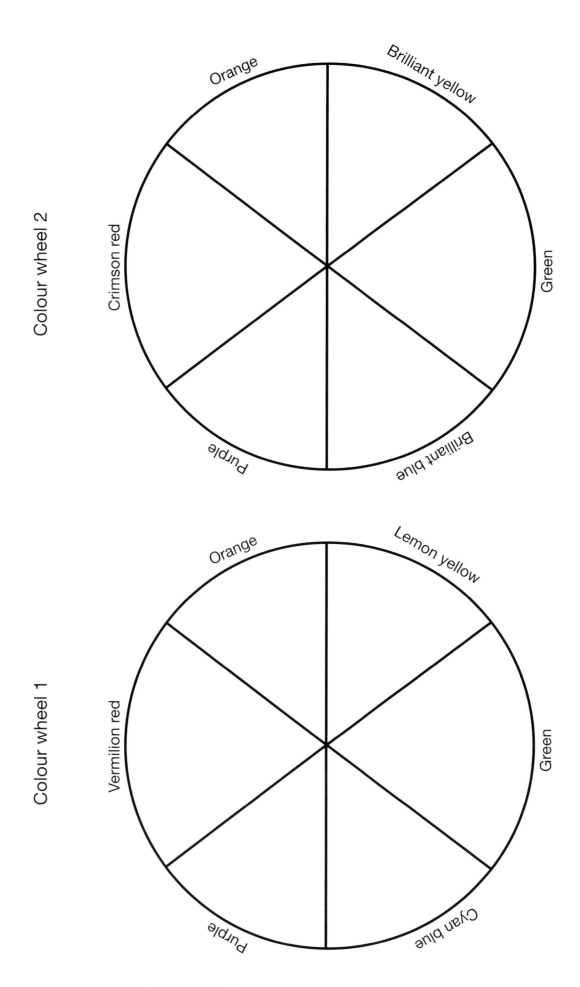

Colour wheel 2

Orange · Brilliant yellow · Green · Brilliant blue · Purple · Crimson red

Colour wheel 1

Orange · Lemon yellow · Green · Cyan blue · Purple · Vermilion red

This page may be photocopied for use by the purchasing institution only.

The extended colour wheel

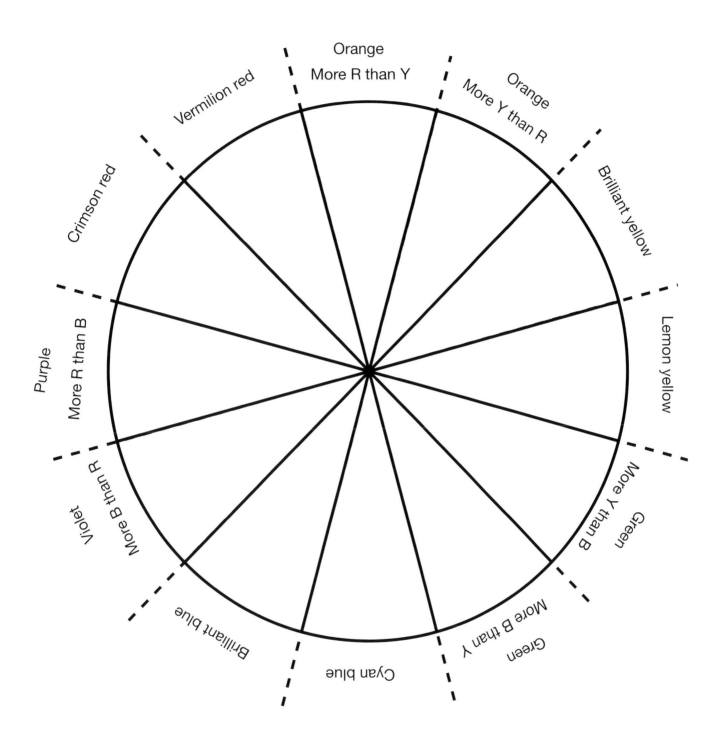

This page may be photocopied for use by the purchasing institution only.

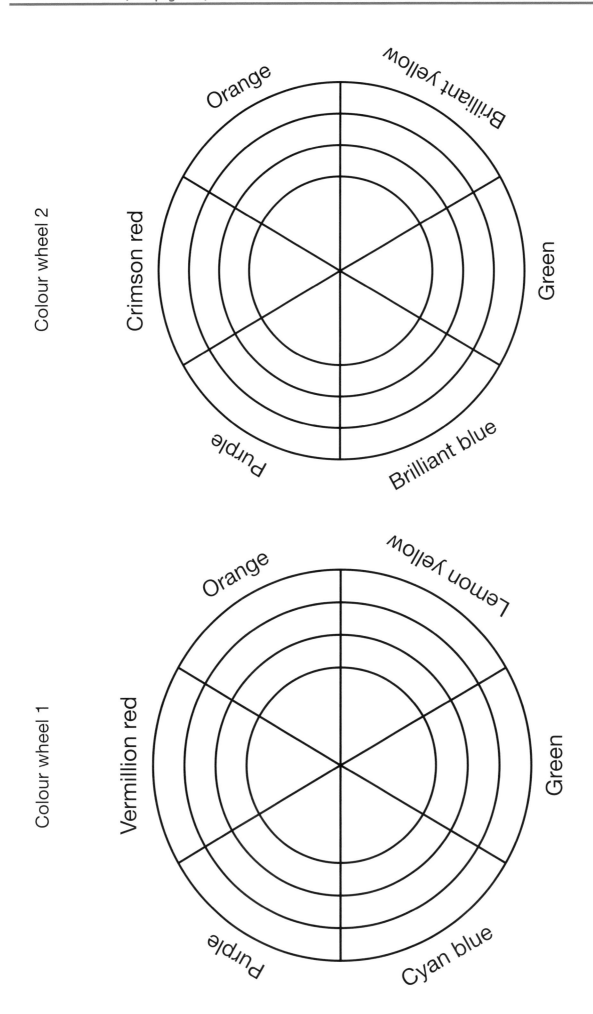

Colour wheel 2

Crimson red

Orange

Brilliant yellow

Green

Brilliant blue

Purple

Colour wheel 1

Vermillion red

Orange

Lemon yellow

Green

Cyan blue

Purple

This page may be photocopied for use by the purchasing institution only.

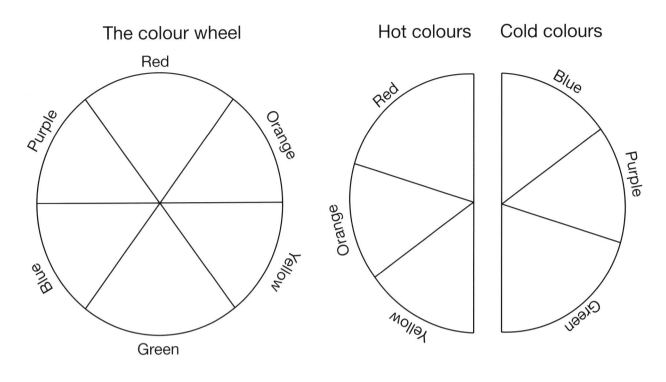

The colour wheel

Red
Orange
Yellow
Green
Blue
Purple

Hot colours

Red
Orange
Yellow

Cold colours

Blue
Purple
Green

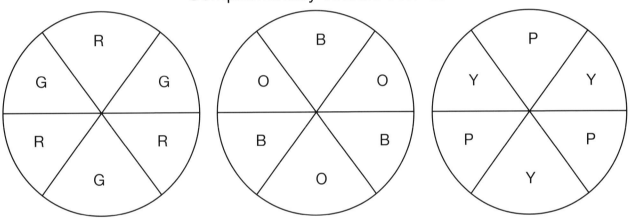

Complementary colours contrast

Harmonious colours go well together

Take any two colours that are next to each other on the colour wheel and make three of each.

For example:
3 greens and 3 blues or
3 blues and 3 purples or
3 purples and 3 reds or
3 reds and 3 oranges or
3 oranges and 3 yellows or
3 yellows and 3 greens or …

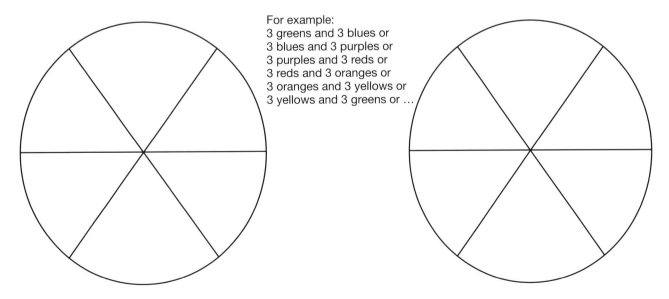

This page may be photocopied for use by the purchasing institution only.

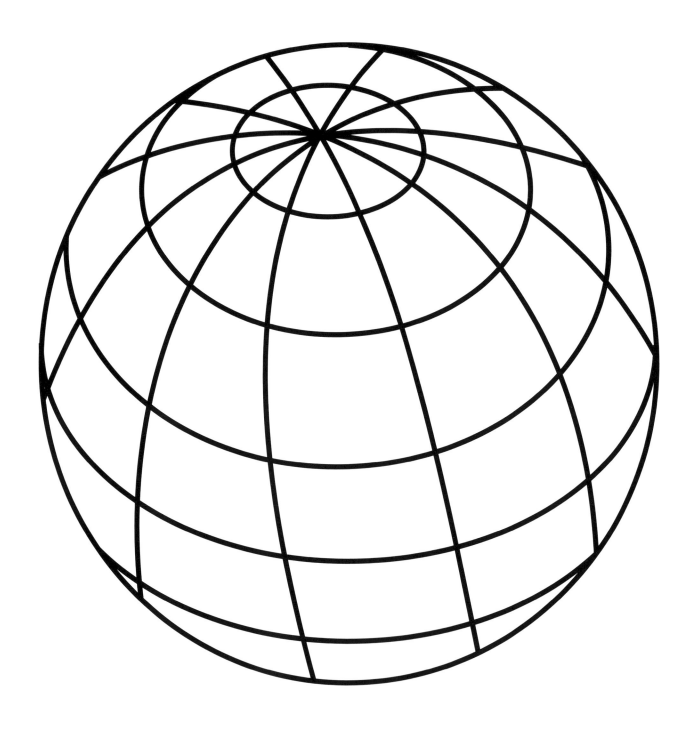

This page may be photocopied for use by the purchasing institution only.

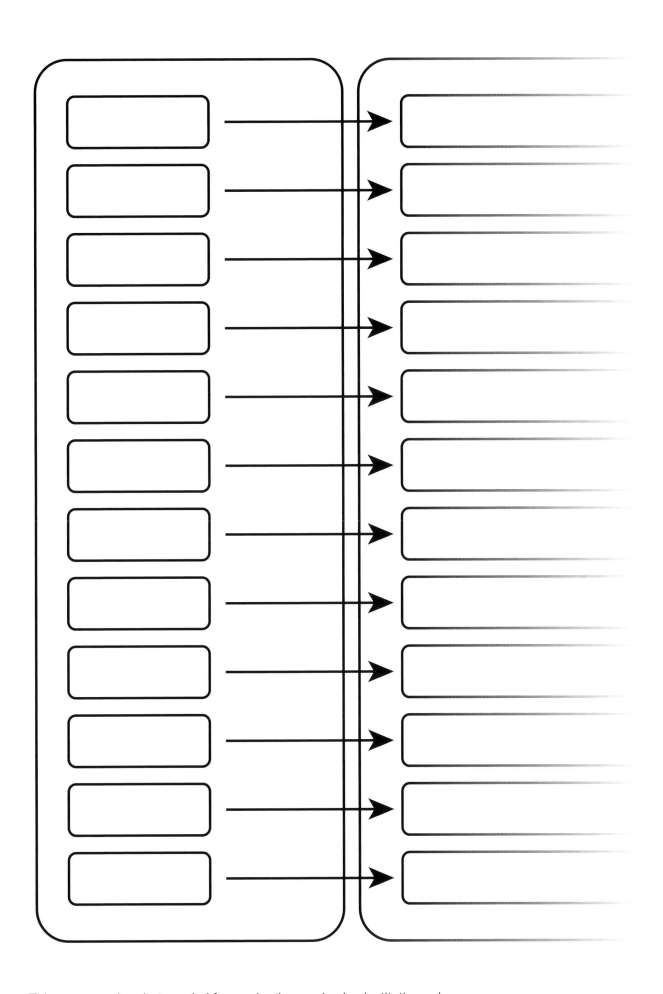

This page may be photocopied for use by the purchasing institution only.

WHITE BLANC	1
GAMBOGEGOMME GUTTE	2
YELLOW OCHRE OCRE JAUNE	3
LEAF GREEN VERT CLAIR	4
HOOKER'S GREEN DEEP VERT DE HOOKER FONCE	5
ULTRAMARINE OUTREMER	6
PRUSSIAN BLUE BLEU DE PRUSSE	7
VERMILION VERMILLON	8
CARMINE CARMIN	9
BURNT SIENNA TERRE DE SIENNE BRULEE	10
VANDYKE BROWN BRUN VAN DYCK	11
BLACK NOIR	12

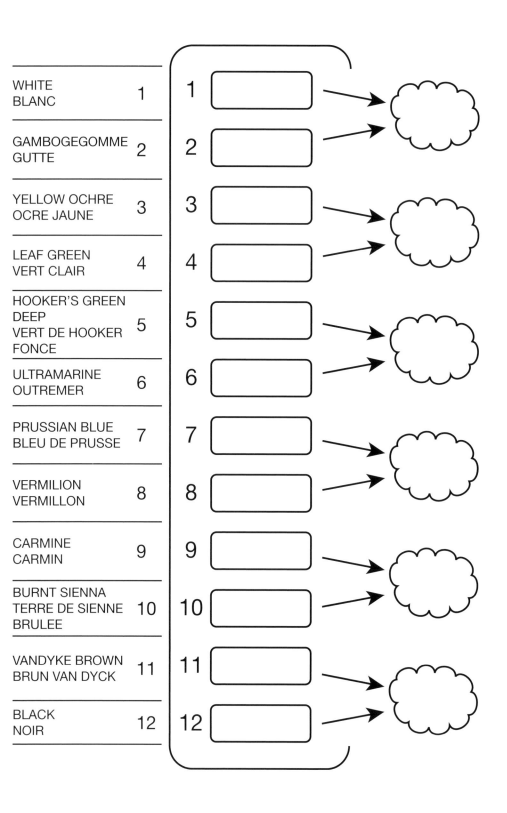

Try some of your own. Record the colours by name or number

Try these colour combinations

10

7

2

12

This page may be photocopied for use by the purchasing institution only.

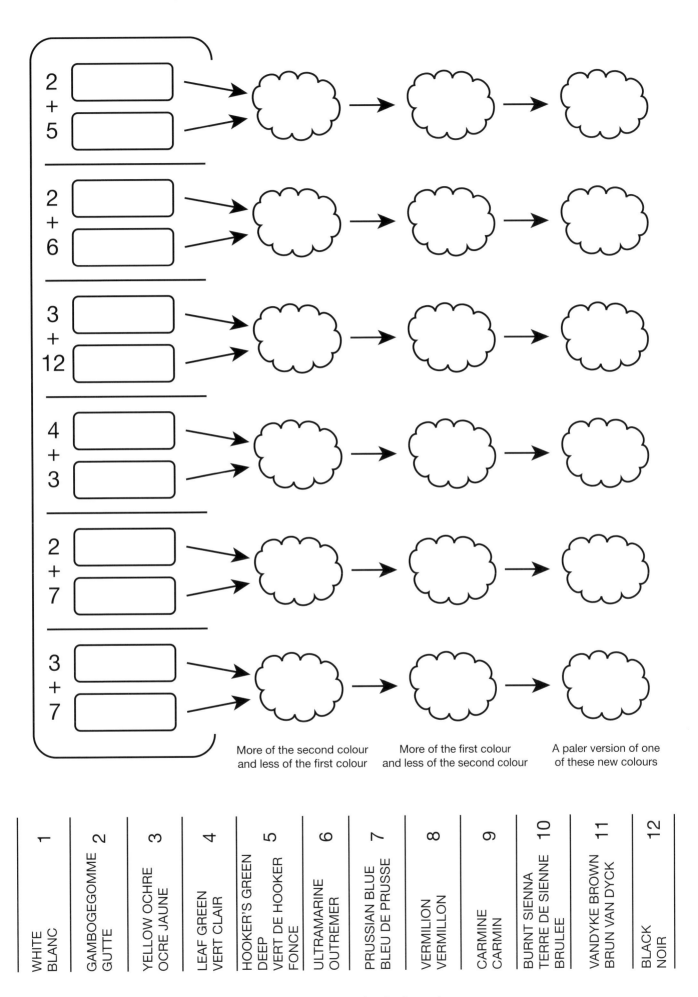

2
+
5

2
+
6

3
+
12

4
+
3

2
+
7

3
+
7

More of the second colour
and less of the first colour

More of the first colour
and less of the second colour

A paler version of one
of these new colours

WHITE BLANC	1
GAMBOGEGOMME GUTTE	2
YELLOW OCHRE OCRE JAUNE	3
LEAF GREEN VERT CLAIR	4
HOOKER'S GREEN DEEP VERT DE HOOKER FONCE	5
ULTRAMARINE OUTREMER	6
PRUSSIAN BLUE BLEU DE PRUSSE	7
VERMILION VERMILLON	8
CARMINE CARMIN	9
BURNT SIENNA TERRE DE SIENNE BRULEE	10
VANDYKE BROWN BRUN VAN DYCK	11
BLACK NOIR	12

This page may be photocopied for use by the purchasing institution only.

This page may be photocopied for use by the purchasing institution only.